I Ranked 10th in the Nation in Total 2012 Presidential Votes on a $5000 Dollar Budget Whats Next? 2016!

I Ranked 10th in the Nation in Total 2012 Presidential Votes on a $5000 Dollar Budget Whats Next? 2016!

Richard Duncan

ISBN:	Softcover	978-1-5035-8819-6
	eBook	978-1-5035-8818-9

Print information available on the last page.

Rev. date: 11/16/2015

To order additional copies of this book, contact:
Xlibris
1-888-795-4274
www.Xlibris.com
Orders@Xlibris.com
719988

Contents

Dedication

Mom and Dad; brother Bob and Kaye

PROLOGUE

In the 2012 Presidential election I received the 10th most votes in the nation and only spent about 5000 dollars on my campaign! Compare this to the millions spent by some candidates that never even make the ballot! This book will explain how this happened and how I propose to help turn around our nation's future! A 2016 Presidential run is underway!

Overall, we probably still have the greatest country in the world. I call this the "good ole U.S.A.". But for years now, numerous sources have discussed how America is in decline or slipping in relation to other countries. Ronald Reagan's son Michael in his book the *New Reagan Revolution*, at page 16 stated as follows:

> "Today, America is on the endangered species list once more. Our economy has been dangerously weakened. Our national debt is unsustainable and still growing. A wave of unfunded entitlement liabilities (trillions of dollars of Social Security and Medicare payouts) is about to hit us like a tsunami. Our military is stretched to the breaking point and dangerously undermined by political correctness. Our government has nationalized the banks, the car companies, and the health care system. We have more government and less freedom than at any other time in our history."[1]

Former President Bill Clinton in his book, *Back To Work In The Future Business*, at the start of Chapter 6 similarly discussed this demise as follows;

> "First, we need to get our game face on. Critics have been betting on America's demise for more than two hundred years

now. They derided George Washington's military acumen, describing him as little more than a mediocre land surveyor. As Lincoln was about to become president, an Illinois newspaper editorial called him a 'baboon' who would destroy the country. Nikita Khrushchev said the Soviet Union would bury us. In the 1980s, the Japanese were going to out-produce and out-trade us into oblivion. I could go on and on. You get the picture. *No one can take the future away from us. But we can take it away from ourselves."*[2]

David M. Walker warns in his book *Comeback America* that the swift, sudden collapse of the Roman Empire could happen again—and it could happen to us:

"Many of us think that a super powerful, prosperous nation like America will be a permanent fixture dominating the world scene. We are too big to fail. But you don't have to delve far into the history books to see what has happened to other once-dominant powers... Great powers rise and fall.... The millennium of the Roman Empire—which included five hundred years as a republic-came to an end in the fifth century after scores of years of gradual decay. We Americans often study that Roman endgame with trepidation. We ask..... are we Rome?"[3]

However, as Bill Clinton states above, many scholars agree that the silver lining to this is that this decline may be prevented by choice or appropriate solutions. Michael Reagan's book states that Henry Kissinger and officials in the Obama administration were and are convinced of America's decline and so their actions turned to managing such decline. The Reagan book at page 40-41 stated as follows;

"Decline is a decision, not a destiny. As Americans, we have the power to choose whether to rise or fall. Ronald Reagan believed that America's best days were ahead of her and his actions in office transformed optimism into reality. So let me say from my heart, the job of the American president is not to manage American decline. The job of the American president is to reverse it."[4]

In fact John F. Kennedy in the 1960's recognized this possible decline and the need to arrest and reverse it. This was stated in Chris Mathews' book *Jack Kennedy Elusive Hero* at page 319 as follows;

> "Jack Kennedy's ultimate trophy had been won by virtue of the truth he'd grasped about his country, one that Richard Nixon had failed to see. 'He had done it driving home the simple message of unease' Time reported, addressing 'the things left undone in the world, where a slip could be disastrous'. The historian Arthur Schlesinger enlarged on the same point in his diary. He wisely decided to concentrate on a single theme and to hammer that theme home until everyone in America understood it-understood his sense of the decline of our national power influence and his determination to arrest and reverse this course. He did this with such brilliant success that, even in a time of prosperity and apparent peace, and even as a Catholic, he was able to command a majority of the voters".[5]

Ronald Reagan, in refusing to accept decline, in his July 17,1980 Republican nomination acceptance speech(as reported in the Investors Business Daily on Tuesday 2/17/2015) stated as follows;

> "We face a disintegrating economy, a weakened defense and an energy policy based on the sharing of scarcity. The major issue of this campaign is the direct political, personal and moral responsibility of Democratic Party leadership—in the White House and in Congress—for this unprecedented calamity..... They say that the United States has had its day in the sun, that our nation has passed its zenith.... that the future will be one of sacrifice and few opportunities.... I utterly reject that view... Those who believe (it) have no business leading the nation"[6].

This book is not intended to debate or elaborate on whether this decline is happening, or what caused it or who is to blame. Many authorities expound on these points. However, I believe all of us as Americans have some role to play in preserving America's opportunities for the future by at least confronting the issues, discussing them and attempting to try to correct the situations before a decline occurs.

Newt Gingerich in his book, *To Save America* however, states the tendency of Americans to turn a blind eye to this issue, retreat into a fantasy world and refuse to face the facts about our nations decline. At page 139 he states as follows;

> "As described in previous chapters, the secular-socialist machine gained power through dishonesty, deceit and deception. But the American people have not been entirely innocent in this process. For years, we avoided hard choices by retreating into a fantasy world where difficult problems simply didn't exist. We thought our country could have wealth without working for it and security without defending it. The inescapable truth is that we have not been honest with ourselves. We are emerging from a pattern of self-deception that transcends partisan and ideological lines. Repeatedly refusing to face the facts, we have been surprised by obvious events that we only missed due to our determination to deceive ourselves. The most devastating example is the 9/11 attack it should not have been a surprise."[7].

Thus, that is why I refuse to remain silent and do nothing and I am writing this book. Chapter 4 herein will discuss briefly our great country as seen mostly from my perspective and life experiences. Also, this Chapter will briefly discuss a few signs which indicate a decline may be taking place in America. Chapters 5 through 7 of this book will discuss briefly what I believe are the causes of or reasons for this decline. I believe all of these have a relation to the structure or nature of our current government which is in need of reform.

In Chapters 8, 9 and 10 I will discuss the crux of my book, "the independent movement or association" which I believe is the solution to America's decline and the best and only way to reform our government. Chapter 11 will conclude this book.

However, before these chapters, I will open this book with Chapters 1, 2 and 3 which will introduce myself Richard Duncan to you the reader. I will take you chronologically from my high school years to the present, and explain some personal events or endeavors which developed my skills and shaped my character.

These events built a foundation for me which led me to become the 10th highest vote receiver in the nation in the 2012 Presidential election. This was done on a total budget of about $5000 dollars! A 2016 Presidential run has commenced at the time of this writing.

CHAPTER 1

DREAMS OF MY FATHER AND MY TEEN AND COLLEGE YEARS

As with President Obama and most children, my dad had a strong influence on me. Rubber bands shot across the postal room at my father at the Chagrin Falls, Ohio post office where he worked as a mail sorter. Before long my dad had co-worker Paul in a headlock, whom he referred to as a "hillbilly". Further tensions intensified when the postal supervisor demanded that dad give him his personal car keys so he could run an errand. Eventually, dad shouted out "I'm not gonna take it!, as the shenanigans continued.

My fathers' standing up for himself, however, got the majority of management against him as they viewed him as a troublemaker. Father referred to most of them as "suction cups". The situation worsened until dad decided to file a grievance with the union. Timidly, he waltzed into the Postmaster's office and remarked "If this continues I will seek redress to the Cincinnati union office". Uninhibited, the Postmaster fired back "go to Cincinnati!" These famous words are even stated today in the Duncan household.

Sure enough, father headed out to Cincinnati one morning with his nephew Charlie by his side for support. With no interstate highways in those days it was more than a days trip. Father easily won his case and the union leaders sat down the management and dressed them down. Things quickly straightened out thereafter. Although I did not realize it until years later, it was hearing about this famous case "go to Cincinnati" time and time again, that eventually planted within me a lifetime personality trait. Stand up to authority abuse!!!!!!!

During, these years, I however was becoming quite familiar with 4 young mop head lads from Liverpool. Us three boys started picking up and strumming dad's Hawaiian guitar in which he often played "near my God to thee". My older brother gave it up as he was more interested in cruising for chicks in his 1967 Chevelle. Before long my younger brother and I were "rockstars" faking guitar and lip syncing at the junior high talent shows. Then we actually learned to play our instruments and sang and got our first paying gig at the wedding of the aunt of a local singer. To this date we still have not seen a penny of it. A gig followed at the St. Edwards church.

EARLY Beatles

In my senior year, a former Cardinal graduate returned from Vietnam and saw me playing keyboards at a Middlefield, Ohio town hall dance. He asked me to join his band and I was taken from a sheltered country school atmosphere and introduced to the wild real world of the post 60's flower child days. I knew nothing about Vietnam but was aware of Woodstock and Jimi Hendrix. We played steadily at the lighthouse nightclub in Eastlake and I got home at 4 a.m. after the gigs. In this band and in a band with my brother I was happy drinking 3.2 beer. Often, our manager bought us the over 21 Boone's Farm or Ripple wine. Although, I was shy, pimpled faced and insecure in high school, music taught me the thrill of being on stage before an audience.

Lutheran East of Course

My mother's early influences on me were sending us boys to the Methodist Church activities across the street and her encouraging me to play basketball. She was a forward at Huntsburg High School so I likewise took to that position as we were both relatively tall. I spent much of my spare time holding a basketball.

We put up a hoop on our garage and we rigged up a decent lighting system for night play. When the weather was bad we went to the neighbor's basketball barn. The 2 baskets were upstairs in this narrow garage. The steps were steep and the rafters prevented many long shots but it did the trick and we could play full court. For a Sunday treat from time to time, the school janitor gave us the keys to the high school gym. He lived across the street so we walked over and he handed us the keys! I doubt this would ever happen in today's world!

I was in the starting lineup on my freshman and junior varsity teams. My biggest game for the Cardinal Huskies was my senior year in 1970 against Lutheran East. They were the favorites to win and did win the championship, largely in part as they recruited players throughout Cleveland. However, we played them at home before a packed house. My friend psyched me up before the game by taking me to a fish fry at the sale barn. He pumped me up so much in the dressing room that I practically strangled a volleyball pole in the locker room by grabbing on to it.

When I got to the floor and the opening buzzer rang, I seemed to be in a daze. Most every ball I threw up went in the bucket. At the end of the game I was carried off the court in a 71-63 upset and I scored 31 points. I accredited my basketball career as being a character or confidence builder throughout my life. I not only made all county and all conference, a study hall classmate wrote a poem about me based on "Casey at the Bat" which I published in the school newspaper.[1] The poem began as follows; "The Huskies just weren't scoring for the Cardinal crowd that night. Behind by more than twenty with no change of luck in site". The poem continued that moments later the bitter fans started to head out the door, but that they wished that Duncan could come off the bench. Their eyes lit up when the coach put him in and the team mates gave him the ball. Duncan tied the score and then he was fouled with no time left. He then shattered the net. The poem ends with "oh somewhere in this happy land, there is a happy spot, where some good teams are winning, and some good teams are not; and somewhere in this wealthy land where basketball began, there's always joy at Cardinal, mighty Duncan did it again". Being a "rockstar" and a famous athlete, I was now ready to conquer the world on graduation from Cardinal High School.

Vice President of the Freshman Class

In the fall of 1971 I was off to Mount Union College with the intention of trying out for the Purple Raider's basketball team.

Election returns

The Elections Committee announced the results of the freshman election in the Student Senate meeting Tuesday: pres., Richard Harr; vice pres., Rich Duncan; sec'y, Nancie Chidester; treas., Greg Jablonski; student Senate representatives, Paula Cope, Candy Disch, and Rusty Smith. 278 freshmen voted, 65% of the class.

DYNAMO

SIT LUX

Published weekly throughout the school year excepting holidays and examination periods. Member of the Ohio College Newspaper Association, and the Associated Collegiate press. Opinions expresed in signed articles are not necessarily those of the College or of this newspaper. Phone 823-4089.

EDITORIAL STAFF

Editor .... Beth Rigel
Associate Editor .... Cheryl Boots
Sports Editor .... Harry Paldas
Business Managers .... Pam Powell, Doug Hebert
Copy Editor .... Cindy Robbins
Layout Editor .... Janet McKenny
Photography Editor .... Dick Kaluchiel

Reporters — Dianne Cope, Paula Cope, Dana Davidson, Sue Hafner, Dave Hetzel, Cindy Kimmel, Laurie Marlatt, Mary Patterson, Marty Peck, Diane Wandsiford.
Columnists — Dareen Adams, Roger Bartley, Cheryl Boots, Paula Climes, Barb Gojewski, Dee Malton, Beth Pittis, Kris Robinson.
Sports Staff — Rich Duncan, Jane Benner, Jim Keppel.
Business Staff — Randi Davis, Debby Grindley, Diana Honaker, Robyn Leiff, Sue Malycke
Copy Staff — Chris Colby, Dianne Cope, Paula Cope, Connie Crim, Bonnie Estes, Joyce Heter, Denise Malone, Sue Malycke, Dee Malton, Beth Ray, Pam Richards, Sue Rigel, Missy Roensch, Sue Sinsabaugh, Linda Slabey, Pam Stevens, Mary Sweet, Lynn Szuch, Linda Thomas, Kathy Wright
Layout Staff — Celeste Ferraro, Linda Impelly, Connie Kramer, Denise Malone, Lynn Szuch
Photography Staff — Becky McClellan, Roberta Infield, Roger Herbst, Liz Zang

After a week of practice I found out that the competition was tough. I also campaigned for vice-president of the class, mostly by hanging out in the girl's dorm McCallister Hall. On election night I went to the student center to see the posted results, and wow! I won! In hindsight, today I now realize the political power women possess! That night I decided to end my basketball career and started a new interest, though it laid dormant for 30 years! Days later the college newspaper reported "The Elections Committee announced the results of the freshmen election in the Student Senate meeting Tuesday: pres. Richard Harr; vice pres. Rich Duncan; sec'y Nancie Chidester; treas. Greg Jablonski".[2] I helped organize a few events but within a few months I transferred out due to the costs of college which

I was taking out loans to pay. I was also coming home most every weekend to play rock and roll with a singer we called Elvis.

Kent State

I chose Kent State University where the politics and lawsuits raged on over the May 4th, 1970 shootings. I was surprised of the notoriety of KSU when I took a trip to San Francisco, and people identified where I was from because of the tragedy. During my college years I got hired as a sub rural carrier at Middlefield's post office, which greatly helped pay for my tuition and living expenses. I eventually majored in geography where I was trained as a city planner. I volunteered in the Houston, Texas city planning department for a few weeks one summer and I quickly discovered a planner's job was largely controlled by politics so my interest shifted more to the private sector and getting a real estate license. Nevertheless, public service and helping others remained of interest and I ended up taking 88 college classes. A significant class I took was called Urban Land Use Policy which drew me into the legal side of city planning.

In April of 1977, I attended a week long seminar at Georgia Tech on Industrial Development Programs, which helped cities to boost their jobs and tax bases.

The Georgia Institute of Technology

This is to certify that

RICHARD AUSTIN DUNCAN

has successfully completed the

BASIC INDUSTRIAL DEVELOPMENT COURSE

conducted by the

Department of Continuing Education

Given at Atlanta, Georgia this 15TH day of APRIL 1977

Director, Continuing Education

President

The attendees applauded me as I was the only one who paid his own way, as they were all publicly funded by taxpayers. On my way to the seminar on that April 10th Easter Sunday morning, my car radio announced that President Jimmy Carter was attending a First Baptist Church in Calhoun, Georgia so I headed into town. After the service, Jimmy greeted the public and when he smiled at me when he shook my hand, I subconsciously felt maybe someday I should go for that job. However, in 1979 I was offered the full time mail carrier job and I took it as $18,000 dollars a year looked very appealing.

That year I finished up with my Masters Degree from Kent State.

Chapter 2

The Reagan 1980's and My Legal Education

In late December of 1980 I was married and still shaken by the assassination of John Lennon. Two lovely daughters, Bridget and Brittany were born in 1982 and 1986. During my spare time after carting around the U.S. Mail to mainly Amish families and spending time with my children, I began to put my college education into practice. I came across a "pro se litigation book" that stated that federal law allowed me to handle my own legal cases. I started studying this and I did many minor cases such as a small claims type leaky roof case. I was finding out I was fairly good at this. Rather than to bore you with the details of petty cases, I will mention 3 three major cases.

Case 1—Car Mechanic

A first significant case involved a mechanic who placed a faulty engine in my mail route car prior to filing bankruptcy. I objected to being included in being discharged on the grounds of fraud and the bankruptcy court and the Federal district court pretty much laughed me out of the courtroom. Finally, the 6th Circuit Court of Appeals reversed in my favor. From this I learned a valuable lesson that even the lower court systems seemed to be influenced by politics or by "who you know or are". Also, it taught me confidence and that for justice to be served it often takes perseverance and a lot of time. Furthermore, I learned the court system hates pro se litigants.

Case 2—You Can Fight City Hall

The next case involves a situation that went on for about 14 years. In the early 1980's I proposed a small apartment building on my parents property in Middlefield, Ohio. The Village officials denied such as the 88.25 foot lot frontage did not meet the 100 foot requirement, a whopping 11.75 feet short. During the next 5 or 6 years I proposed, revised and withdrew plans to the Village's boards and litigated about 5 lawsuits therefrom.

In one of these early 1980's cases, I quickly learned a lesson from a local Judge. He scolded me "quit banging your head against the wall and get a lawyer". It was clear they did not want me handling my own case despite the fact that it was legal, that I was well prepared and courteous and well versed on the law. Though I admit I may have been a bit overzealous in the number of applications I filed, I believe the Village got angry as they were not able to bully me around. Therefore, they then resorted to turning the media on me by making me look like a trouble maker. One case ended up in the Ohio Supreme Court in 1986. My father and I went to the hearing in Columbus, Ohio. I won on the legal points I raised and it turned out to be a landmark case. Basking in my glory I decided to take a few years off.

However, in 1988 I decided to try a civil rights zoning case in Federal Court in Cleveland to which I felt I was legally entitled to file. The Village was furious claiming these issues were already litigated and Duncan was up to no good again. The District Court ruled for the Village. In December of 1991 the Village sought to collect about $18,000 in attorney fees under a civil rights statute. The same Judge ruled for the village and the village once again turned to the media. The entire town seemed to "eat it up" and they essentially tar and feathered me.

The Village attorney garnished my bank accounts for 18,000 dollars. I researched the law on the matter and fought for my life on appeal to the 6th Circuit. This was the Court I won on in the car mechanic case. In March of 1993, I was backpacking on a Eurail train pass in Europe, when my father read to me on the phone a letter from the Cincinnati appeals court that reversed and vacated the frivolous ruling! My trip suddenly got more enjoyable. In July of 1993, on remand to the Cleveland District Court the Judge reversed his decision and ordered the return of my money.

The lesson I learned from this saga was that if you dare to challenge city hall, you can expect retaliation in many forms, including adverse media coverage and any legal tool they can find. This is so despite the fact that all of my dealings were professionally handled, and by right under the authority of our American Constitution. The Village continually made it appear that I was wasting the taxpayers money. The Village attorney reported to me in a letter that the Village spent $86,000 in attorney fees defending cases I filed. Of course this attorney stated that I "forced the Village to expend" these fees. Did the Village ever consider that if the Village settled with me or if the 11 foot variance was granted they could have used most of this money to benefit the taxpayers, for example to pave a road or to build basketball courts, etc? Instead their attorney made out like a bandit. This illustrated to me the recklessness common with government officials when they are spending money that belongs to others. However, to this day the negative effects of this saga are still felt locally in government circles who refuse to own up to being responsible and mature in their positions. For example, in 2013, I applied for a zoning inspector job in neighboring Burton Township. At the start of the interview, I was rudely greeted by a Trustee where he stated in front of a public meeting in a childish manner, "Here is the troublemaker"!

However, outweighing all of this negativity were the benefits. When the Ohio Supreme Court ruled in my favor in 1986, they corrected Ohio law they were wrongly applying and established the "Duncan factors" on area variances.

> While existing definitions of "practical difficulties" are often nebulous, it can safely be said that a property owner encounters "practical difficulties" whenever an area zoning requirement (*e.g.*, frontage, setback, height) unreasonably deprives him of a permitted use of his property. The key to this standard is whether the area zoning requirement, as applied to the property owner in question, is reasonable. The practical difficulties standard differs from the unnecessary hardship standard normally applied in use variance cases, because no single factor controls in a determination of practical difficulties. A property owner is not denied the opportunity to establish practical difficulties, for example, simply because he purchased the property with knowledge of the zoning restrictions. *Kisil, supra,* at 33; cf. *Consolidated Mgmt, Inc.* v. *Cleveland* (1983), 6 Ohio St.3d 238.
>
> The factors to be considered and weighed in determining whether a property owner seeking an area variance has encountered practical difficulties in the use of his property include, but are not limited to: (1) whether the property in question will yield a reasonable return or whether there can be any beneficial use of the property without the variance; (2) whether the variance is substantial; (3) whether the essential character of the neighborhood would be substantially altered or whether adjoining properties would suffer a substantial detriment as a result of the variance; (4) whether the variance would adversely affect the delivery of governmental services (*e.g.*, water, sewer, garbage); (5) whether the property owner purchased the property with knowledge of the zoning restriction; (6) whether the property owner's predicament feasibly can be obviated through some method other than a variance; (7) whether the spirit and intent behind the zoning requirement would be observed and substantial justice done by granting the variance. See, generally, 3 Anderson, American Law of Zoning (2 Ed. 1977), Variances, Section 18.47 *et seq.; Wachsberger* v. *Michalis* (1959), 19 Misc.2d 909, 191 N.Y. Supp. 2d 621.
>
> The appellant, village of Middlefield, asserts that, in spite of the board's finding that the Duncans had not suffered an "unnecessary hardship"

This case is widely cited as the precedent today and I frequently get favorable comments for arguing this landmark case.[1] On August 4th, 1993 Herb Luxemborg sent me a 100 dollar check for having the courage to fight city hall where he wrote "strike a blow for liberty and property"!

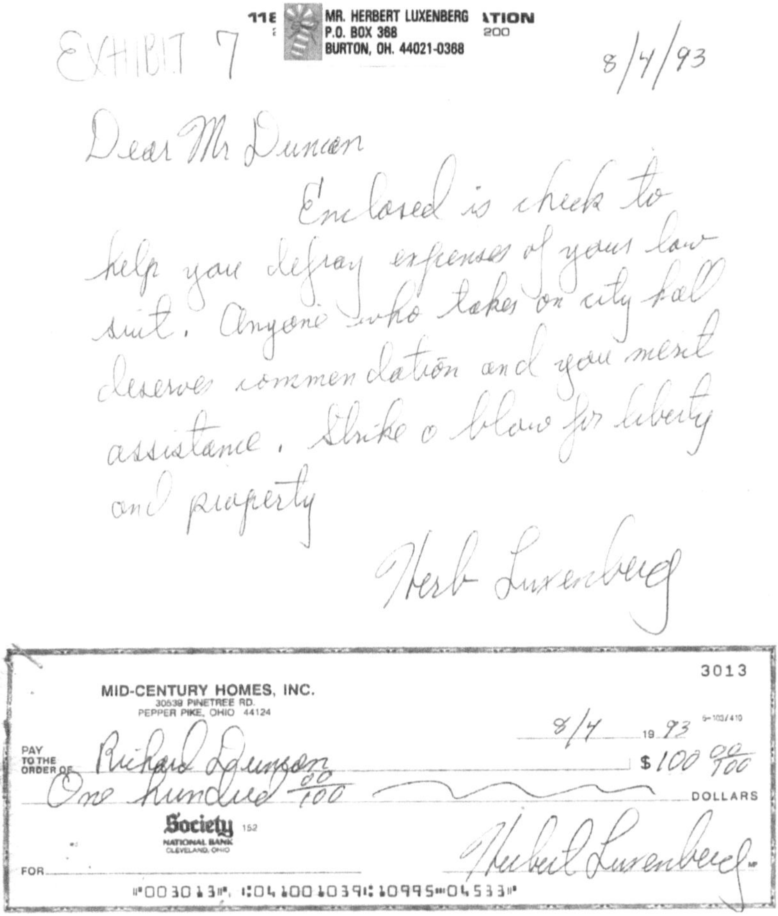

EXHIBIT 7

MR. HERBERT LUXENBERG
P.O. BOX 368
BURTON, OH. 44021-0368

8/4/93

Dear Mr Duncan

Enclosed is check to help you defray expenses of your law suit. Anyone who takes on city hall deserves commendation and you merit assistance. Strike a blow for liberty and property

Herb Luxenberg

3013

MID-CENTURY HOMES, INC.
30539 PINETREE RD.
PEPPER PIKE, OHIO 44124

8/4 19 93

PAY TO THE ORDER OF Richard Duncan $100 00/100

One hundred 00/100 DOLLARS

Society National Bank
Cleveland, Ohio

FOR

Herbert Luxenberg

I also got personal satisfaction by knowing I was right and taking a stand on an issue, even if it was not politically correct or popular. Sam Adams and John Hancock were also well known for their efforts on politically unpopular matters! Well in the least, I defended an issue just like my father when he "went to Cincinnati!"

Case 3—Visitation

A third case I handled pro se was an uncomfortable situation regarding my children's visitation rights. After my divorce was finalized, a motion was filed to move my children to a western state. I at first hired an attorney on this matter due to its seriousness. At the hearing to allow a temporary move out of state, several witnesses testified that I was a terrible father to my children. In my opinion I also felt questionable deceptive techniques were used. I presented the truth as to how I was a great dad. To my surprise, even my lawyer made harmful comments to the court about me. He stated "many think Richard is a pain in the neck, he is..... even to his lawyer". Wouldn't you know it, the next day I got a call from my attorney who told me that the referee let the kids move and that it would be a waste of money to try to appeal it. They did move and I was devastated but I smelled a rat.

I felt my attorney conspired with the judicial system to send my kids away. I fired him and once again blew the dust off my "pro se" law books. I pointed out at a hearing before the Judge a visitation violation at Christmas that resulted in me not seeing my girls for 5 months and I showed him photo after photo of my numerous vacations with my children and how I never missed a visitation right. My pastor and dad testified also.

Finally, the Judge ruled for me and ordered the kids back home to Ohio "forthwith". When they still did not return, the bailiff called me and suggested that I file a change in custody so I did. The kids were back within a few days.

I blamed the time away from my kids and this waste of time and money on this lawyer. I filed a bar association complaint against her alleging numerous violations of her professional behavior. I later sued her for legal malpractice for the deception I believe she put before the Court. But try winning a case where the judge is in the same bar association and you are an outsider as a pro se litigant. She was also president of the bar. You can imagine how far these cases got.

Chapter 3

My Run for the White House

In the 1990's I enjoyed time with my children and for a few years we put together a mostly "girl band" which we called "East Blvd."

In 1993 I bought a Eurail train pass and I back packed for a month in Europe, sleeping mainly on the night trains. I was so fascinated by the experience that I did it again one year later. In total, I visited about 22 countries, including Russia and Morocco, Africa.

During the early 1990's on our monthly summer visitation, we went to Baltimore's children museum. There was a young girl named Lucy Baverova who had a letter at the museum looking for pen pals. She was from the Republic of Czech and my girls and her started writing each other. During both of my Europe trips I stayed at their home in Kutna Hora and I was treated like a king. In the year of 2011, my daughters and I went to their house to meet their pen pal, who by now was married.

In 2004, Brittany, my youngest daughter, was having trouble with her senior year government class so I stepped into help her. This triggered a thought which went as far back when President Jimmy Carter shook my hand in Calhoun, Georgia, that I may want the job as U.S. President. I also now had my Masters Degree, trained to help out the future of urban residents. So here was my opportunity, so I got the forms for a write-in candidate in Ohio for President. High school classmate Robby Cubertson, who now lived in Texas agreed to be my 2004 vice president. The Cleveland Plain Dealer printed an article on us which I felt was only intended to be a humor story. People chuckled when I made our political promise that "were going to lose". The reporter stated "No candidate ever uttered truer words and that the duo's odds of winning Ohio run longer than a political speech". Even Vice Presidential candidate Cubertson surprised me when in a telephone interview with the reporter he stated "Don't waste a vote on us"[1]. The negative comments did not bother me because at the same time I got the write-in forms, I took out the 3A forms needed to get my name printed on the ballot in 2008. Immediately I started to gather a few of the 5000 signatures I needed to run as an independent candidate. I was nervous for awhile and I got many smirks and was laughed at occasionally aloud; "You President?" When the 2004 election results came in George W. Bush buried me, I got 17 votes. Oh well, my costs were only a hand painted sign.

The 2008 Presidential Race

I wasn't too worried about my 2004 defeat as I was already leaning toward my 2008 race against Obama and McCain. On weekends, holidays and out of town sporting events such as the Ohio State Buckeye games I slowly trudged toward the 5000 needed signatures. I was asked to leave some businesses as they claimed I could not solicit there. Not discouraged I proceeded to my next destination where ever I could find voters. Eventually, I got the 5000, then 6000, and soon I had double. After I got about 13,000 signatures, I drove down to the Secretary of State's office in Columbus to turn them in for verification.

However, weeks beforehand disaster almost struck as vice president Cubertson called me and told me he wanted off the ticket as he was getting internet coverage not to his liking. He was a staunch Republican and he was being viewed as betraying his party, like Teddy Roosevelt forming the Bull Moose party. He reluctantly agreed to sign off on the forms which officially pulled him out of the 2008 race. His letter filed August 18, 2008 stated as follows;

"In the 2004 General Election I was a candidate for Vice President on the ticket with Richard Duncan as the President. This letter is meant to be my official request to be removed for consideration as the candidate for Vice President or any other political position in any election in Ohio in 2008. Respectfully Robby C. Cubertson Timber Briar Circle, Houston, Texas 77059."[2]

I quickly got a voters list of independent candidates from Mercer County, Pennsylvania, which was about an hour from my home. I made hundreds of calls looking for a new vice president. I preferred an African American female so I could appeal to many minority groups but none seemed interested. However, I did find a Baptist preacher from Ferrell, Pennsylvania who exuded with enthusiasm to better our nation.

I was certified for the ballot on my daughter's birthday on September 19, 2008 and I started to get a few invites to a few functions. This time the Cleveland Plain Dealer did two serious articles on me, one where they interviewed me and photographed me in front of Moses Cleveland's statute, who founded Cleveland. A second article highlighted 3rd party candidates in the race. My college newspaper at Kent State University also did a nice article on me entitled "Kent State Graduate eyes White House, Ohio native offers an alternative to McCain and Obama options"[3]

Other than these articles, I got the feeling that many other newspapers did not appreciate me competing with the "big dogs". The Columbus Dispatch completely omitted me. Nevertheless, on election night I got 3902 votes and was quite happy. I spent about 5000 dollars on my campaign compared to millions as spent by Obama and McCain. I was proud I got the 12th most votes in the nation! Plunderbund's website applauded me and commented as follows;

"Mr. Duncan…. turns out to be a pretty interesting guy…. didn't have a big campaign website or any advertising… and yet he still managed to get almost 4000 votes. Compare that to Alan Keyes, a nationally known conservative politician, who only pulled off 31 votes in Ohio this year. Richard Duncan has shown us that our political system really does allow anyone to run for office—even the highest office in the nation"[4]

The 2012 Presidential Race

Once again I obtained the 3A forms to try to oust Obama in 2012. I previously went from 17 votes to nearly 4000 so I figured I was heading in the right direction. I once again collected about 13,000 signatures to make sure I had a cushion on the 5000 needed. This time I wanted to try to get votes in states other than Ohio so I wrote away for the 49 other state requirements, mainly as to being a write in. Generally, I met the requirements for about 20 to 25 states by filing forms, collecting some signatures and paying a few filing fees. On August 27, 2012` the Secretary of State's office once again certified me to have my name printed on the ballot. This time I was the only independent in Ohio. I also got a few invites this time nationwide from Florida, Kentucky, Maryland and Indiana. By now I had a simple website from my Sams Club membership.

RICHARD A. DUNCAN

FOR

PRESIDENT OF THE UNITED STATES OF AMERICA

My name is Richard A. Duncan, and I am running for President in 2012. I am 59 years old. I reside in Aurora, Ohio (Portage County) near Cleveland. I graduated from Kent State University in 1979 with a Masters Degree in Urban Geography where I prepared myself for a career as a city planner. I specialized in governmental land use controls and the development of New Communities such as Irvine, California; Columbia, Maryland; and Reston, Virginia.

I was a write-in candidate for U.S. President in 2004. I also ran for U.S. Senator in 2006 and received 803 write-in votes. I was elected Vice President of my freshman class at Mount Union College in 1971.

In 2008, I was on the ballot for United States President and received 3,902 votes. The Federal Election Commission certified me as the 12th highest vote getter in the nation.

I completely fund my own campaigns and thus can represent my constituents fairly, rather than favor heavy campaign donors.

I have practiced real estate sales under my license I have held since 1976, worked for the U.S. Postal Service, worked as a security guard and have invested in rental dwellings. I remodeled a home into my current campaign headquarters in commercial area in Middlefield Village.

In 1982 and 1986 God blessed me with two precious daughters, Bridget and Brittany. Now that my children are adults I want to devote time toward helping the public and to improve the quality of lives in the future. I completely fund my own campaign, and thus have no ties to anyone except the needs of the American people.

Outlined below are my skills, qualifications, and experiences, and my platform:

I. Skills, qualifications, and experiences

From the time I began my Master's Degree training for a career as a City Planner in the early 1970's until the present date, I have continued to enhance and hone my qualifications toward my goal of eventually becoming a public servant to improve the quality of life of all Americans.

These are as follows:

- 1971- I was elected Vice President of my freshman class at Mount Union College (Alliance, Ohio)
- 1975- I worked in the Houston, Texas City Planning Department as a volunteer.
- 1976- I attended an Industrial Development Seminar at Georgia Tech, where the focus of the program was how to attract business into a governmental jurisdiction.
- During my college years, I traveled to all the states except Hawaii and collected urban land use and transportation plans.
- My major project for my Master's Degree requirement dealt with the examination of the comparison of various governmental/land use controls and results which accrued therefrom (zoning as opposed to more relaxed methods).
- During my college training I visited and extensively studied the development of New Communities such as Irvine, California; Columbia, Maryland; and Reston, Virginia. These were cities built virtually from scratch.
- During the last 25 years, I have successfully argued many issues in the judicial system pro se where I was not represented by a lawyer (four of these cases were in the Ohio Supreme Court).
- In 1986, I was the Plaintiff in the landmark Ohio zoning case of Duncan vs. Middlefield (1986); 23 Ohio State 83. In this case, I successfully argued before the Ohio Supreme Court what would become the correct law on area variances in Ohio.
- In a 1991 case, the Federal U.S. Sixth Circuit Court of Appeals reversed an attorney fee award against me; after determining that Duncan's (my) filed claims surrounding the above mentioned 1986 cases were proper.
- In 2005, in [The State Ex Rel] Duncan v City of Mentor City Council, 105 Ohio St 3d 372, 2005; the Ohio Supreme Court agreed with me and overturned the Court of Appeals and Mentor, stating that genuine trial issues existed on whether the City's restrictive covenants on my property may have contributed a compensable taking.
- In 2007, I ran for Aurora City Council and was excluded from the ballot, as the elections board claimed I did not live in Aurora. The Ohio Supreme Court affirmed that, based on the evidence I presented before the board. Two years later, I presented comprehensive evidence, including 9 years of municipal tax forms, that proved I was an Aurora resident, and I made the ballot.

In summation, I believe these past cases have been very valuable to me helping out the public in the future; as it demonstrates that if I have a public issue that I believe in, I have the tenacity and persistence to make it a reality.

- In 1992 and 1993 I traveled overseas two seperate times and visited 22 countries;

mainly in Europe as well as visiting Russia and Africa. While there, I studied urban land use patterns and rode over 10,000 miles on the magnificent Eurail train system. In April of 2011 I again traveled the Rail Europe system in about 7 countries. While in Paris I studied the Paris Rive Gauche which is Paris's last large undeveloped mixed use development neighborhood (innovatively elevated above railway tracks).

- In 2009, I visited the site of the United States Supreme Court case Kelo v. New London, where the City government of New London, CT succeeded in implementing its economic development plan objectives (despite eminent domain).

Memberships

- I am a current member of the Center for Law and Justice, which argues the preservation of Christian viewpoints.
- I am a recent 4 year member of the American Planning Association.
- I am a current Vice Chairman of the City of Kent Board of Building Appeals. Kent City Council recently appointed me for a second term.

I was Director of the Geauga County Maple Festival's Battle of the Bands from 2003-2009.

I have a private business of being an election consultant in which I assist candidates and issues to get on the ballot (the most recent being Ohio's Senate Bill 5 referendum in November of 2011).

During my contact with the public in this election consulting business and in my past election runs, I have personally spoken to over 25,000 United States Citizens. These encounters have been instrumental in formulating my platform, which is detailed below in the Platform Section.

II. My Platform

One of my top priorities is homeland security vs. terrorism and the resolution of the wars in Iraq and Afghanistan. I believe militarily and strategically it is beneficial to be in that region to monitor terrorism, but the cost of lives and tax dollars must be curtailed drastically, or at least attempted to be cut back. I believe we must maintain a presence in these areas to prevent safeheavens for terrorist groups from building up as recently occurred prior to September 11th, 2011. However, we must try to prevent invasions of these countries where we are left with the task of nation rebuilding. We as Americans have a nation building chore in the U.S. which I will highlight below.

Federal Jobs and Economic Boost Act (The Duncan Plan)

Secondly, the goal of creating new jobs and preserving the ones we have in this country is crucial to me. I believe I am equipped to take on this goal due to my aforementioned qualifications, training and background in city planning principles. The public benefits are immense (social, economic, moral) from the governmental actions, means or tools which I detail below:

The major tool I would use is to propose rehabilitation projects for American cities. I would propose legislation that would target large scale distressed or blighted urban areas that have substandard housing and overcrowded conditions. Such areas will be proximate to existing central business districts. A federal or state board will administer such projects. These projects would be guided by carefully executed development plans, a common exercise of urban planning.

Corporations and businesses will be aggressively sought to locate there-in, and will benefit financially from various inducements such as favorable land prices or leases, tax breaks, etc (as previously mentioned, I attended a seminar on these industrial development programs).

However, they would be required to:
1) Employ only documented US citizens at reasonable wages, and
2) Offer health care plans to its employees at reasonable terms.

In addition to replacing these run-down areas with new industrial and commerce parks; new schools and parks, new utilities, infrastructure, streets, and affordable housing will be built. These new communities (similar to the ones I studied during my Master's Degree training) will become more beautiful, healthy, spacious, well-balanced, and carefully patrolled. Improved transportation systems will be implemented within, and high-speed rail projects (similar to what I experienced in Europe) will connect the projects state-wide.
The green movement will be integrated within each project, and the environment will be protected. Energy savings in gasoline will result due to the close proximity of jobs to housing and mass transit.
In addition to the added employment opportunities, health care plans, and the improved physical design and live-ability of our urban areas which will result from these projects, our governmental budget will move further towards being balanced.

Due to the resulting economic rejuvenation, property tax values in these areas will rise, and this money can be used for the school systems. Additional taxes can be collected and devoted to the government's general revenue funds from the worker's incomes (income taxes), from sales taxes, use taxes, corporate and franchise taxes, and other miscellaneous taxes.

A further budgetary advantage of such projects is that by putting people to work (and thus providing families with income), expenditures to the government social agencies

will be cut (for example, in Ohio the Department of Job and Family Services is allocated 20 billion dollars for 2010).
Medicaid and medical charity assistance opportunities (as mentioned earlier, corporations will be required to provide health care), housing assistance, and welfare and unemployment programs should be reduced.

By providing people with jobs, this should help to reduce crime and reduce prison populations, thus reducing appropriations to our judicial/correction systems.

The United States Supreme Court has consistently upheld the power of the US legislatures to enact and implement such projects as long as the public purpose is reasonably advanced (aforementioned Kelo v New London case).

An obstacle to these projects will be overcoming many state laws which hinder such projects by confining them to severely blighted areas (Ohio's SB 167). I believe a judicial challenge could overturn or mitigate Ohio's law.

The City of Kent, Ohio, has taken a lead with the Kent Transit Plan in its downtown area, which is an admirable example of such a project, in an area of non-blighted conditions. I urge all Americans and City Planners to visit Kent, Ohio and experience the fabulous job the Government and the citizens have partaken in in a joint public and private partnership to improve our future. .

In summation, I will use 3 main tools to boost and revitalize America's job and economic conditions:

Tool 1- Launching major urban renewal projects in our major cities. These will be targeted to crime and blighted areas closely accessible to our central business districts and involve high density projects.
Tool 2- Commencing an aggressive industrial or business development program which encourages corporations, etc., to locate in these revamped areas.
Tool 3- Improving intra-city public transportation systems with links between cities by a high-speed rail system similar to those I experienced in Europe.

Equal Education
A third issue of concern to me is to assure equal opportunities for all children to receive an education. Despite ones present status, if they want to invest the effort, their American dream must be an achievable vision!!!!!!

In regards to improving school finances, I would like to investigate whether recommendations from the DeRolph v State of Ohio Ohio Supreme Court cases on school funding have been followed. Although improvements likely have been made, I would like to be assured that property taxes can no longer be the primary means of providing the finances for a thorough and efficient system of schools.

Ohio's new evidenced-based funding plan needs to be thoroughly examined.

Other Issues
Other issues of concern to me are:

- A firm and fair immigration policy which deters illegal crossings of our borders. If a need is shown to increase the quotas for a particular nationality of people, this should be reviewed, but jobs for our citizens and our budgets should not suffer (tax dollars on health care and schooling for illegals). Employees should be penalized if they hire these non-U.S. employees.
- The continued development of alternative energy sources, particularly exploring our resources on and off shore. Careful attention will be committed to preserving our treasured natural resources.
- Providing a national health care program for the middle class who need it most.
- Restoring morals in our country, preserving the right to life, and maintaining God and the right to religion as constitutionally possible.

.Our federal deficit will be firmly addressed as covered above which may also include spending cuts in areas of government which are repetitive and wasteful. Cuts in tax rates will likely occur to help spur the economy by giving citizens and small businesses more money to invest. We can no longer put our expenses on our childrens credit cards!!!!!!!!

I respectfully request that you, the voters, give to me the incentive to pursue my journey of improving the quality of lives of Americans.

Thanks for the support! RICHARD A DUNCAN

On election night I went to my campaign party at my daughters. We turned on the television to view the early returns, and my daughter excitedly spoke out "dad there is your name"! Initially I dismissed this as perhaps another Duncan running for office in another state. But sure enough the votes were starting to roll in for Richard Duncan the Presidential candidate. By 8 p.m. I surpassed my 2008 total and by midnight I was close to 12,000 votes. I was later certified with 12,557 votes. Within that total 37 were from Kentucky, 15 in Maryland and 3 were from Florida. This ranked me 10th in the nation! Obama and Romney were the top vote receivers. Libertarian Gary Johnson and Green Party candidate Jill Stein were 3rd and 4th. Virgil Goode of the Constitution party and Roseann Barr of Peace and Freedom were next in order. Ranking 7th and 8th were Ross Andersen of the Justice Party and Thomas Hoefling of the American Ind. Party. Beating me by 600 votes was Randell Terry as an Independent. Fascinating to say the least! Once again, I only spent about $5000 dollars on my campaign!

The 2016 Presidential Race

After a long hard fought battle I rested and took 6 months off and then got the itch to try it again. However, the Ohio legislature, the Ohio General Assembly had a different plan. Apparently, after seeing that I was a serious candidate and that I was starting to get more votes, the 2 party political machine started to toughen up on the ballot access rules for independents. This should not be shocking as most if not all of the legislative members are either Republicans or Democrats. Also, in a later chapter of this book, I indicate how the U.S. Supreme Court has continually warned the State of Ohio to abandon their monopoly on the two party system! After I collected about 800 signatures, I got a letter from the Secretary of State telling me of Senate Bill 47 which essentially restricted my signature gathering time down to one year (this rule applied only to independent candidates like myself). I had previously collected my signatures over about a three year span. Thus, I stopped gathering signatures until I got within about one year from the 2016 general election.

I felt this would be very difficult to get my 5000 valid signatures within such one year period, especially as I collected all of them on my own. One reason I did this alone was because a major theme of my platform was a low cost campaign where it cost me about 5000 dollars total! Contrast this to the multimillion dollar campaigns of modern day Presidential elections! This point will be elaborated on in a later chapter of this book.

I therefore decided to challenge this law as I felt they were discriminating against me as an independent candidate and I felt they were suppressing my free speech right to appeal to other voters who wanted to associate with candidates who held political views other than those of republicans or democrats. I researched the law on this matter and in November of 2013 I filed a "pro se" suit in the United States District Court in Columbus. This case is still pending in the Courts. I started collecting signatures to get on the 2016 Presidential ballot in mid-July of 2015 but whether I can get 5000 valid signatures is not yet determined. In the early going I got a rocky start in a few places where I went to collect signatures. At the Franklin County, Ohio fair I was escorted off the grounds by the Director in a glorified Kubota golf cart with a canopy. This bureaucrat was really important! At the St. Marys festival in Chardon, Ohio a local policeman spotted me with a clipboard and before you know it I was surrounded by 4 officers, and followed off the church property. Clipboards can be very dangerous weapons!

Chapter 4

The Good Ole U.S.A.

As was stated in the earlier chapters, I traveled to Europe in 1993 and 1994. However, prior to this time I had not traveled outside of the continental U.S.A.. Therefore, for about 40 years I took for granted the liberties and comforts that we as Americans enjoy.

However, my trips to the Czech Republic, where Communism had just fallen, gave me a feeling that this country was very backwards economically. The trains were old in appearance and they ran on rickety rails. However, a bag of potato chips only cost 7 cents, even if they were a bit greasy. On my first trip to Paris, I bargained with the hotel keeper on the price and she scolded me saying "you Americans do not know how good you have it". In Moscow and in Morocco I never felt totally at ease as I was scared about being assaulted due to lack of security. I also viewed terribly impoverished areas often from my train window. Perhaps the strangest event was when I went to get my train ticket at the Saint Petersburg station to go to Moscow. The station ticket lines were 30 people deep and almost no one spoke English. When I found a lady who spoke English, she came back to me and told me I would have to go through the mafia for a ticket. I obviously, had no other choice, but the cost was reasonable. When communism fell, the mafia took over. So, the European trips showed me their cultures were different from the U.S.A., but not drastically different.

In April of 2014 I took a month long trip around the world where I visited Asia. This is where I noticed bigger cultural differences from our country. In Delhi, India when I arrived at their sparkling new airport, I noticed a lot of guards with intimidating assault weapons. From there, I took an immaculate subway at 5 a.m. down into old Delhi. At the crack of dawn I ascended from the filthy stairways to the stinch, massive crowds, hundreds of rickshaw taxis and debris and trash everywhere. You could barely cross the street without getting run down. Animals of all kinds shared the streets. I'm sure all of India is not like this. Open urination was common and a homeless man took his trousers off and tried to pleasure himself in public. It was common for people to go number 2 at the train station beyond the tracks in clear eyesight.

On the first day I arrived I wanted to get my train tickets to the Taj Mahal and to Mumbai. A security guard told that the International Ticket Office had moved to another location, so he motioned for a taxi to take me there free of charge. I should have suspected something. This ticket office was on a small dusty side street and this agent told me my tickets would be ready in about 4 hours. So for a fee of 20 dollars the taxi driver offered to give me a personal tour of Delhi. I reluctantly agreed.

As time went on, I began to feel I was being scammed, so I got out my map and started looking for the nearest subway station. I told the driver to take me there, and I jumped out and paid him. Due to the exchange rate this driver made a days wages, but I was relieved to get away from the situation.

I managed to get to my Ramada Inn in Gurgaon that afternoon which was very stylish and oil Arabs (as far as I could tell) paraded through the lobby. In sharp contrast, when I looked out my 11th story window I saw wandering sacred cows, piles of trash and dilapidated apartments. Down the street people washed up publically in a running stream of water.

The next day I found the real international ticket office and I read a sign warning the public about how I was swindled. When I got my tickets, I was happy as I avoided paying 3 times my cost by jumping out of the taxi. We had a 3 hour train ride to the Taj Mahal in the daylight. Here I noticed the extreme poverty and dilapidated housing conditions. Mumbai was a lot more modern than Delhi and more commercialized.

From Mumbai, I flew into Hong Kong and took a bus to one of the entry gates into mainland China at Shenzhen. Soon I found myself enclosed in a wall to wall crowd. Though it was a holiday, the subways were most always jammed with people. Before I left Shenzhen I took a day trip out to the Long gang District on the train. I found mile after mile of factories and businesses located along the train stops. Conveniently located nearby were tall skyscrapers of dormitory housing where the Chinese workers lived during the week.

Most everywhere in China I found the Chinese people very helpful, friendly and courteous. From Shenzen I took a train west to Nanning and from there I took a bus south into Vietnam. My growing up in the Vietnam war era and knowing many Vietnam vets, like my cousin Leonard Smallwood inspired me to visit Hanoi for a few days. Motor cyles and scooters dominate the narrow maze like roads.

I was very careful not to get ran into, but I never once witnessed an accident to my amazement. The streets were lined with 20 foot wide business shops selling anything imaginable, except duct tape, which I desperately wanted. Electric lines draped telephone poles like a bowl of spaghetti.

Merchants devised any way of making a living, including ladies on bicycles loaded down with goods to sell.

I visited many military museums out of respect of our veterans. Hanoi was a fascinating place to visit and is on its way back to prosperity but it sure reinforced my appreciation of the U.S.A..

With no convenient train routes back into China I had no choice but to fly Vietnam Airlines up to Chengdu. I was unable to get an express train to Shanghai due to that they sell out quickly with a population of over one billion in China. So I had to forfeit visiting Chengdu and headed out on a night train to Wuhan, which is in central China. I had a 12 hour layover. All day long I never saw anyone who was not Chinese, and almost no one spoke English. From Wuhan, I took a night train to Shanghai. The subway system was high tech. The city was commercialized and oriented toward tourist dollars. Overall, this is a wonderful city as was Pudong. I was scammed by a female graduate student where she deceivingly took me to a tea ceremony with her friends.

She presented me a 250 dollar bill for the entertainment I never wanted. I told her I would pay 50 dollars just to avoid a dispute. From there I went to Beijing the capital. It was here that the communist government was very noticeable with the presence of the police and military everywhere.

I asked the Chinese if they could own property and the answers were mixed. Perhaps, while the rules are trending toward this, I believe long term leases are the norm, keeping the title to property in the Communist state. When I visited Tiananmen Square, I certainly felt this was not the place to test out my free speech rights in America.

Thus, particularly from my past travels, I now realized the major comparative advantages in freedoms and economic conditions of the U.S.A. over other nations. Thus, many great opportunities exist here in America. Look at the freedoms I had in my "pro se" court cases as set forth in Chapter 2 and my runs for the U.S. President as set forth in Chapter 3. In contrast, in China independent candidates for public office have been ruled illegal, according to a newspaper article I read and that the communist government handpicks the communist candidates for you. This New York Times article stated as follows;

> "The Chinese authorities appear to be restricting attempts by a handful of citizens to run in local legislative elections as self-proclaimed independent candidates, stating that such candidates are illegal and that no one can run for office without first clearing a series of procedural hurdles....... In practice, candidates are largely handpicked by Communist Party officials and committees, and outsiders are frequently discouraged from seeking office."[1]

I believe Dinesh D'Souza, in many of his books, corroborates my opinion on this point. In his book *America, Imagine A World Without Her* (2014), D'Sousa, who left India in 1978 as a teenager, stated in America that your destiny is not predetermined but is constructed by you. He stated at page 38 as follows;

> "In India, as in most places, life happens to you; in America, I came to believe, life is something you do. 'Making it' doesn't just mean succeeding. It means making your life. I came to America alone, without family or relatives here, and without money. In America I have not only achieved my ambitions; I have outpaced them. I originally intended to become a corporate executive of some kind; instead I found my true vocation as a writer, speaker and filmmaker. I came to discover America, and here in America I have discovered myself. In this country I have not only found success; I have also been able to write the script of my own life. In America your destiny isn't given to you; it is constructed by you."[2]

D'Souza in his book accredits America's success to 1) its democratic self-government where the people control the rulers (and not the other way around) and 2) the freedom of entrepreneurs to be minimally regulated. It is this self governing democratic formula which has set a successful example for many nations to follow. Moreover, America's focus on the entrepreneur has produced the most inventive and entrepreneurial society in history which has benefited not just business-owners but workers and ordinary people. Historian Daniel Walker Howe points out:

> "Already by 1815 Americans were better fed and in better health than their English counterparts. Between 1830 and 1950, America had the fastest-growing economy in the world. By the mid-twentieth century, the American economy was so productive that a nation with around 5 percent of the world's population accounted for one-fourth of the global economy"[3]

WARNING SIGNS OF DECLINE

So what are a few of the warning signs which could show a decline in America. A few of these will be set forth briefly below;

The National Debt

One of the main indicators which shows America may be in decline is our massive national debt which exceeds 19 trillion (and rising by the minute). Bill Clinton, in his 2011 book entitled *Back to Work in the Future Business* states that this 19 trillion is on borrowed money from foreign countries such as China and Japan, and that hopefully interest rates will not rise forcing a higher cost to service the debt which would leave less money for future investments in our future. Clinton states he regrets that the past 1981 to 2009 U.S. Administrations stopped paying back their borrowings or balanced their budgets at page 35 as follows;

> "What did we do with the money? We didn't invest it in new scientific and technological research, in rebuilding our manufacturing base; instead we consumed it, in ways that distort our economy today and cloud our children's tomarrows"[4]

Newt Gingerich, in his book *To Save America* highlights the inevitable adverse result of higher taxes if these debt and spending problems, which are largely caused by medicaid, medicare and social security, are not curtailed. At page 186 he states as follows;

> "Do you want an economic system in which you pay most of the money you earn to the government, and the government gives you back benefits on terms and conditions decided by politicians and bureaucrats? That is not the America of freedom and prosperity we have known for more than 300 years. That is the vision of Karl Marx."[5]

Lack of Good Quality Jobs in America

While this factor tends to fluctuate monthly to yearly, or changes depending on who's report you read, it is obvious that the quality of America's jobs have declined recently. In a September 1, 2014 article in Barrons, Gene Epstein stated that this job situation has led to many people refusing to even look for work. This stated as follows;

> "The job market has made a comeback over the past year, but the American labor force hasn't, and the prospects don't look good. Work seems to be on the wane in the U.S., with worrisome consequences for economic growth. While the unemployment rate slipped to 6.1% in June—its lowest level in six years-the percentage of adult American workers who are actually in the workforce is at its lowest level in 36 years, with no rebound in sight."[6]

Janet Yellen, the Federal Reserve Chairman, in an October 18,19th 2014 Wall Street Journal article, stated the disparity in income and wealth results of the past few decades for those at the top and the majority as follows;

> "The past few decades of widening inequality can be summed up as significant income and wealth gains for those at the very top and stagnant living standards for the majority, she said".[7]

The need of America to be strong economically for domestic and national security interests, has long been recognized as a sign of future success, as John F. Kennedy recognized. In his book called *Elusive Hero* Chris Mathews stated at page 296 as follows;

> "The United States needed to be strong economically, Kennedy declared, not just to maintain the American standard of living but because economic strength buttressed our fight against Communists. 'If we do well here, if we meet our obligations, if we are moving ahead, I think freedom will be secure around the world. If we fail, then freedom fails. Are we doing so much as we can do?', he asked an anxious country. 'I do not think we're doing enough'."[8]

Decline in Nuclear and Military Power

Dinesh D'Souza, in his book, *America, Imagine A World Without Her,* stated 3 obvious indicators of decline. The first 2 corroborate my viewpoints where he states at page 5 "first, the American economy is stagnant and shrinking relative to the growing economies of China, Russia, India, and Brazil" and at page 6 that "second, America is drowning in debt". Thirdly, on page 6 and 7 D'Souza states that America is also declining in terms of nuclear and military power as follows;

> "Finally, America is losing its position in the world. The Obama administration is downsizing our nuclear arsenal when other nations are building and modernizing theirs. Under the START Treaty, America has gone from several thousand nuclear warheads to a limit of 1,550. In 2013, Obama proposed cutting that number even further to around 1,000, and he has said he intends getting rid of nuclear weapons altogether. Whether America's nuclear impotence will enhance world peace is debatable; that it will reduce America's military dominance is certain."[9]

Besides nuclear hegemony, America is also relinquishing its hegemony around the world, especially in the strategically and economically vital Middle East, according to political scientist Fawaz Gerges. In his recent book *Obama And The Middle East* he writes America's;

> "Influence .... is at its lowest point since the beginning of the cold war in the late 1940s....... America neither calls the shots as before nor dominates the regional scene in the way it did..... We are witnessing the end of America's moment in the Middle East"[10].

D'Souza states that the growing power of other emerging countries such as China and Russia has also restricted America's impact in Asia, Europe and South America and thus America seems on the way to becoming a feeble giant, a second Canada.

Thus, we are beginning to show serious signs of decline in America. The next few chapters will state what I believe are the main causes or reasons for such decline.

Chapter 5

Too Big of Government and Socialism

I believe one of our biggest problems in America today is that our government has grown out of control in size.

In his review of Richard Epstein's 2014 book *The Classical Liberal Constitution,* Andrew Napolitano states the often debated theory of too much government, or libertarian legal theory (also known as classical liberalism) which places the individual over the state as sovereign. This was reported in Barrons on August 2, 2014 as follows;

> "It claims Jefferson's mantra that the best government is the least government, and regards the state as merely one of many institutions voluntarily created by individuals in order to preserve our freedoms. The classical liberal argument reflects the historical truism that the Constitution was written in order to create a limited central government whose core purposes were to facilitate a common defense against outside forces of violence and to maintain a free market among merchants and consumers in different states. At the same time, the express intention was to keep the government off the people's backs by recognizing that areas of human behavior—what we call natural rights—are largely immune from government authority".[1]

Lee Edwards in his review of Heather Cox Richardson's book, *To Make Men Free* comments as follows as to how much government is the proper amount(as reported on 9/20 and 9/21, 2014 weekend edition of the Wall Street Journal);

> "What is the proper role and extent of government? The Founders recognized the darker side of human nature and strove in the Constitution to forge a balance between liberty, for which they fought a revolution, and order, which would protect the rights of all, not just the most powerful or the wealthiest".[2]

This "darker side of man theory" which is recognized as an argument for limited government was quoted by Ann Coulter in her book *Demonic* at page 143 as follows;

> "You could ask every signatory to the Declaration of Independence—indeed, you could poll every colonial American—and not one would have said the problem with King George was that the rights of man had slipped his mind. Rather, our founding fathers believed—as Madison wrote in *Federalist 10*—that men are more likely to oppress another than to 'co-operate for their common good'. In particular, he said the power to tax created the greatest temptation to 'trample on the rules of justice', because increasing someone else's taxes 'is a shilling saved to their own pockets'".[3]

Former President George W. Bush on page 23 of his book *Decision Points*, illustrated the abuses which generally occur from too much government, that he learned from his experience of living in China after his college graduation as follows;

> "China's experience reminded me of the French and Russian revolutions. The pattern was the same: People seized control by promising to promote certain ideals. Once they had consolidated power, they abused it, casting aside their beliefs and brutalizing their fellow citizens. It was as if mankind had a sickness that it kept inflicting on itself. The sobering thought deepened my conviction that freedom—economic,

political, and religious—is the only fair and productive way of governing a society."[4]

When Thomas Jefferson and later James Madison proposed that a Bill of Rights be added to the Constitution, Alexander Hamilton objected. Hamilton said enumerating such rights was 'not only unnnecessary' but could even be dangerous. He asked, "Why declare that things shall not be done which there is no power to do?". He added "why for instance should it be said that the liberty of the press shall not be restrained, when no power is given by which restrictions may be imposed?" Hamilton was concerned that specifying a list of restraints on federal power might encourage the government to claim unwarranted authority in areas where no specific restraints were listed.(see The Federalist, No. 84)[5]

As a result of this overgrowth of government many Americans do not trust it anymore. This was stated by Martin Conrad in the March 23, 2015 issue of Barrons at page 40 as follows;

"Today, few Americans are content with our government. Most are frustrated and don't trust a government they once admired to do the right thing. Trust in government has dropped a stunning 50 percentage points in 50 years, from over 70% to about 20%."[6]

Often overlapping with the "big government" issue discussed above is the movement toward "socialism". This is also referred to as anti-capitalism or anti-imperialism.

This idea of socialism also adversely affects American's money, property and pursuit of happiness, which was initially expounded upon by the Founders such as Thomas Jefferson who gained this inspiration from John Locke's *Second Treatise of Civil Government.*[7] To Jefferson and the other Founding Fathers, the pursuit of happiness entailed the ownership of property or estate as Locke put it. When big government takes your property and redistributes your wealth to others it steals your happiness.

Socialism is often attributed to George Soros and his 'shadow party' which is believed to exert influence on U.S. Foreign policy and U.S. Elections. As reported in Human Events is as follows;

"Soros is Obama's principal patron. He created Obama. An Obama presidency will be a Soros presidency...... George Soros has stated repeatedly and explicitly that he views the

> United States and its capitalistic ideology as a threat to world peace. A consistent pattern, both in his political giving and in his philanthropic endeavors, is to press for policies whose only possible effect will be to bankrupt the United States and end the reign of the U.S. Dollar as the world's dominant exchange currency. Soros wishes to replace the U.S. Dollar with a global currency, issued by a global bank."[8]

Dinesh D'Souza has written extensively on the subject and he states that this is an intentional plan to make America fail as they believe America deserves to fail. In his book *America, Imagine A World Without Her,* at page 4 he states as follows;

> "It should be emphasized at the outset that the domestic champions of American decline are not traitors or America-haters. They are bringing down America because they genuinely believe that America deserves to be brought down."[9]

D'Souza credits Barack Obama as the modern day main architect of this plan as he believes Obama feels the wealth of the west was obtained by theft. This is stated at page 10 of his book as follows;

> "Obama's presidency can be summed up in the phrase, 'Omnipotence at home, impotence abroad'. Domestically, the Obama Democrats have been expanding the power of the state and reducing the scope of the private sector. Internationally, they have been reducing the footprint of America in the world."[10]

D'Sousa states in his first book *Obama's America* that he believes this anti-colonialism is a third world ideology which was accelerated during the Vietnam War and was fueled by those living in impoverished nations who observed rich nations invading, occupying and looting poor nations. He believes this theory has been developed by many anti-colonial radicals in America such as Barack Obama Sr., former communist Frank Marshall Davis, the domestic terrorist Bill Ayers, the Palestinian scholar Edward Said, the self-described Brazilian revolutionary Roberto Unger and the incendiary preacher Jeremiah Wright. D'Sousa states Obama Jr. schooled himself on this theory at Columbia and Harvard Law School and honed his talents on the streets of Chicago as a community organizer.[11]

However, it is an undisputable fact that capitalism drove America to prosperity in the past, despite many abuses. A recent book called *Out Of Poverty Sweatshops In The Global Economy,* by author Benjamin Powell, reveals that this prosperity of capitalism still today outweighs the frequent adverse affects in today's world economy This was reported by Gene Epstein in his book review in Barrons March 2, 2015 as follows;

> "As grim as Third World factory jobs appear to our First World sensibilities, they represent tangible progress to people of the Third World rationally committed to bettering their lives, just as our immigrant ancestors voluntarily coped with harsh conditions that were better than those they had left behind."[12]

On a personal level I can also attest to the struggle of big government or socialism in regards to private property rights. For 3 and a half decades, starting in the early 1980's I started studying every U.S. Supreme Court case I could find related to zoning or land use as I had my college Masters degree training in urban planning and real estate. I will review a few of these major cases below.

Generally, governments are given much leeway in their actions to protect the interests of the public as a whole. This is often called the presumption of validity. On the other hand, to protect the individual property owners from government abuse from this police power our founding fathers adopted the Fifth Amendment which stated that property could not be taken unless just compensation is paid. It must be emphasized that they can take private property for public use, however, if they do so they must pay you for it!

One of the earliest cases was *Pennsylvania Coal Co. v. Mahon* 260 U.S. 393. Takings have always been recognized for example when governments physically occupy or possess a private property. This 1922 case however was different in that it involved a regulation and the question was whether the Koehler Act could actually be similar to a physical taking? The Court's ruling coined the famous statement that yes if it "goes too far" compensation must be paid. However the Court in recognizing the government's obligation to the public gain stated "government could hardly go on if to some extent values incident to property could not be diminished without paying for every such change in the general law". Such case established this balancing act that must take place between government and private rights. In this case a taking was found.

The next big case came in New York City in 1978 called *Penn Central Transportation Co. v. New York City.*(438 U.S. 104). It involved the owners attempt to build atop of the Grand Central terminal. The Court held there was no taking as the owner could continue with its present use whose return, it conceded was reasonable. The Court set forth that it has been unable to develop any "set formula" for determining when justice and fairness require that economic injuries caused by public action be compensated by the government but it set forth several factors that have particular significance that must be considered. It listed "the economic impact of the regulation on the claimant, and particularly, the extent to which the regulation has interfered with distinct investment-backed expectations; ......so too, is the character of the government action, where a taking may more readily be found when a physical invasion by the government occurs rather then when an interference arises from some public program adjusting the benefits and burdens of economic life to promote the common good". The Court ruled an ad hoc balancing of these factors must take place.

The next case of significance was *Agins v. City of Tiburon* (447 U.S. 255). This 1980 case setforth a 2 prong takings test. However, after 25 years of confusion in regards to this test, the Court abrogated one of these prongs.. This case also started a series of 3 Supreme Court decisions that failed to reach a decision on the merits of the cases as the cases were not ready to be decided. The Court defined the "ripeness rules" which prescribed that property owners must first give the government a chance to 1. arrive at a final decision and to 2. give back just compensation before they can file suit. In this case Donald Agins failed to even submit a plan for his proposed development on his property which proved fatal to his case.

In 1987 the Supreme Court ruled in *First English Evangelical Luthern Church of Glendale v. County of Los Angeles, California* (482 U.S. 304). Here it finally decided the lingering or remedial issue which was the main question that could not be decided in the prior 3 cases subsequent to *Agins*. The Court held that a temporary regulatory takings requires compensation be paid just as it does in any other taking. In other words, when it has been found by a court that "the governments activities have already worked a taking of all use of property, no subsequent action by the government can relieve it of the duty to provide compensation for the period during which the taking was effective". The Court remanded the case to the lower court to determine if the owner was deprived of all economic use. The dissent predicted that a "litigation explosion" would occur from this ruling. In my opinion the ruling was helpful as it warned city planners to be careful in crafting legislation affecting private property! The Court however stated that "normal delays in obtaining building permits, changes in zoning ordinances, variances and the like are not before us".

In 1992 the Supreme Court ruled in the case of *Lucas v. South Carolina Coastal Commission* (505 U.S. 1003). In this case the State of South Carolina in a regulation effectively deprived David Lucas of building any home on his coastal property. The Court ruled that to deny a property owner of all economically viable use of his property constituted one of the discrete categories of regulatory deprivations that requires compensation without the usual case specific inquiries into the public interest advanced in support of the restraint. In other words, when all use is denied on a private property by the government, the factors set forth in the *Penn Central* case discussed above did not have to be weighed. The Court in siding with property rights rejected the dissents discussion of a governmental gain by stating "since such a justification can be formulated in practically every case; this amounts to a test of whether the legislature has a stupid staff. We think the takings clause requires courts to do more than insist upon artful harm prevention characterizations".

Ten years later in the 2002 case of *Tahoe-Sierra Preservation Council, Inc. v. Tahoe Regional Planning Agency* (535 U.S. 302) the Court addressed the above issue not decided in the above *First English* case on normal delays. In this case the government imposed a moratorium on building while the land use planners reviewed different options. The Court ruled that even a total taking of private property during this period did not constitute a categorical taking such as in the *Lucas* case as discussed above as governments must not be pressured into making quick ill conceived land use decisions. It did set forth a standard that delays longer than one year should be viewed with skepticism. The Court stated that the length of the delay must be viewed as another factor under the *Penn Central* weighing test.

In 2005, the Supreme Court ruled in the case of *Lingle v. Chevron U.S.A. Inc.* (544 U.S. 528). This is the case that overturned the *Agins* case stated above by ruling that no longer a taking could occur when a regulation "does not substantially advance a legitimate state interest." It stated that this was more of a substantive due process inquiry.

Thus, as can be seen from the above cases, there has been alternating rulings by the Supreme Court where they have held for the government's power to regulate for the public as a whole and then held for private property owners under the Fifth Amendment. I agree with most of these rulings and their reasoning setforth in support. I also believe that due to the strong language of the Fifth Amendment, individual private property rights have held their own from governmental abuse.

I also agree with the Supreme Court's other 2005 ruling which has set off a storm of controversy. This was the case of *Kelo v. New London* 545

U.S. 469. This Connecticut city used their power of eminent domain to transfer land from one private owner to another private owner to further economic development. In a 5-4 decision the Court held that the "general benefits a community enjoyed from economic growth qualified private redevelopment plans as a permissible public use under the takings clause of the Fifth Amendment." I visited New London years after the decision and found the community very nice and the development plan rationally based. I viewed the site where Suzzette Kelo's pink house was originally located and later relocated.

However, many pundits were outraged from the Supreme Court's ruling. As reported 10 years after the decision in an editorial commentary by Scott Bullock and Nick Sibilla in Barron's on July 6, 2015 is as follows;

> "In the decade since the Kelo case, 47 states have enacted legislative reforms or issued court decisions to protect property owners from eminent-domain abuse. Working with activists nationwide, the Institute for Justice has saved more than 16,000 homes, businesses, places of worship, and other properties from demolition".[13]

I disagree with the criticism. While 16,000 homes may have been saved, the downside of this is that if development had been permitted to proceed under carefully formulated governmental plans, perhaps 160,000 to a million homes or businesses may have been created. Also, if the government was permitted to proceed as was allowed in New London, perhaps many of America's businesses would not have relocated offshore to such countries such as China, India and Vietnam.

The Supreme Court in *Kelo* justified such takings as a public use as it stated "as with other exercises in urban planning and development, the city is trying to coordinate a variety of commercial, residential and recreational land uses, with the hope that they will form a whole greater than the sum of its parts". In my Land Use Policy case in 1976 I advocated this type of development as a better alternative to zoning. I wrote a paper titled "Large Scale Community Development—A Land Use Control of the Future". Also, my Masters Degree thesis like requirement covered this topic. Certainly, we must try to exercise this type of development if it keeps jobs in America!

Chapter 6

The Republican/Democrat 2 Party System Problem

Another big problem leading to America's decline is the current procedure in place, and which has been used for the past century, to solve our nation's problems or challenges. This is called the 2 party system.

The Watergate incident which led to President Nixon's resignation is a glaring example of how far both of these parties will go to win an election, regardless of whether the public or voters win. Bill Clinton, in his book called *Back to Work in the Future Business* talked of this polarization problem on page 11 as follows;

> "I believe the challenges we face, which are tough enough on their own, are made even more difficult by the highly polarized, deeply ideological political climate in Washington. It is an almost alien environment to me now, because what I do today---in my foundation, in the Clinton Global Initiative, and in Haiti—is a world away from Washington's political wars"[1]

Long time Congressman Joe Lieberman in November of 2013 visited Roanoke College and in a speech he stated the lack of compromise as follows;

> "Politicians, he said, have become so loyal to their parties and unwilling to compromise that Congress has become wildly unproductive. He said the past two years have been the least productive of all. 'I don't miss Congress' he said. Lieberman retired earlier this year from his long-held Senate seat. He said there are problems, the biggest being the national debt, that are going unresolved because of the gridlock. 'Our leaders in Washington have stopped compromising with one another', he said, adding that compromise is what led to the formation of the U.S. Constitution and the creation of Congress itself. George Washington 'warned that loyalty to factions... would overcome loyalty to the nation' Lieberman said" (this article was reported by Tiffany Holland).[2]

Steve LaTourette, a veteran House of Representative Congress member has always prided himself on being a problem solver. However, he recently retired to take a lobbying job as he felt there was no place for compromise anymore like existed with Ronald Reagan and Tip O'Neil. From his experienced viewpoint in a March 6th, 2013 Record Publishing article by Conner Howard he stated as follows;

> "Today, what drove me out the door was that people basically want to fight about everything. If an idea was thought up by a Democrat and your a Republican, you have to say it's a horrible idea and vice versa. It limited my ability, in my opinion, to be an effective problem solver because nobody was interested in solving problems"[3]

However, I would like to point out from my experience that this partisanship exists not only at the national level as noted above, but it is possibly as obvious in local politics. I will cite an example of such. In 2014 I ran as an independent for the office of County Commissioner in Portage County, Ohio, where almost all of the politicians are democrats. However, the seat I ran for was occupied by a female republican. In 2010 she narrowly beat out the democrat opponent, thus being the first republican elected since 1992 to the county commissioner post. She therefore served with 2 other democrats.

In addition to this partisan difference, she filed a lawsuit against her former boss democrat County Prosecuter who fired her as an employee. As reported by James McCarty of the Cleveland Plain Dealer on 9/23/2011 she claimed he fired her because "he disapproved of campaign material she drafted in a bid for a municipal judge seat. She had prepared a campaign advertisement critical of one of her opponents, then the Ravenna Mayor, who later won the election. In the ad, she stated she was not a member of the 'Ravenna Good Old Boys Corruption Club'".[4] The Prosecutor demanded she not publish the ad. She did not satisfy his request and so she was fired in 2009.

To qualify for the ballot, I had to get about 500 signatures so I talked to about 1000 Portage County voters. In circulating my petition, I quickly learned there was a great amount of tension between the 3 commissioners. I asked one gentleman in a grocery store to sign my petition and he stated he was her father. He stated how much friction she had taken from the democrats. One morning I rode the elevator in the Administration building and the 2 riders were her and the present democratic commissioner Kathleen Handler. I confronted her as to why she did not sufficiently answer a question I asked her earlier on the phone. When I once again got an unsatisfactory answer, Kathleen Handler rolled her eyes in dismay.

In early 2014 she resigned as commissioner to take a job with the Ohio Turnpike Commission. From this limited evidence, my gut feeling was that the democrats pressured her to resign her position as she was a republican in a democratic county, who refused to go along with the democratic "good old boys club". Obviously, such can't be proved.

I knew my chances were slim as an independent so when the results came in I did not win as expected, but the democratic winner Nickie Kind accredited me on learning of her victory by stating in the newspaper "that third party made a difference in the race". From the advice of former President John Kennedy I was partially relieved I did not win the election. In Chris Mathews' book *Jack Kennedy, Elusive Hero,* he stated at page 201 as follows;

> "The fact is Jack Kennedy had no intention of staying involved in townie politics. He knew it was like quicksand: you got into the fray, picked sides, made enemies, and could never free yourself from it. He now needed to reengage himself in national politics."[5]

Despite this often viciousness of partisanship and the "quicksand" you can often encounter in local politics, I have had a positive experience in Portage County as being appointed to the City of Kent's Board of Building Appeals. I have been reappointed twice and currently serve as its vice chairman. Not once have I experienced any partisanship in this city, which is Portage County's largest.

The City of Kent has done a remarkable job in a public-private partnership with Kent State University on redeveloping its downtown. Its 100 million dollar facelift has created 1600 jobs, provided a Kent State University Hotel and Conference Center and provided a new transportation facility in downtown Kent. Many new businesses such as restaurants, bars and specialty shops serve the area. This is vastly different from when I frequented the dingy downtown area in my 1970's college years.

I appreciate living in Portage County and my hometown City of Aurora as the people are "down to earth" and the countryside is charming. Perhaps, if the County public officials put aside their partisanship issues and concentrate on serving the public's future interest, wonderful things such as Kent's downtown project would happen elsewhere in the County!

Chapter 7

Money Influence

A further problem leading to America's decline is the influence of money. This age old problem, often called "quid pro quo" is defined by Wikipedia as follows;

> "Something given to you or done for you in return for something you have given to or done for someone else"[1]

But the influences of money can be traced from the colonial times to modern times. Zephyr Teachouts' book *Corruption In America* as reviewed by Sarah Chayes of the Wall Street Journal in the September 27-28, 2014 weekend edition, reveals this ancient inherent problem of receiving private gifts while serving public office. This controversy occurred when Benjamin Franklin accepted a diamond studded snuff box from Louis the XVI upon departing his post as ambassador in Paris. The colonial delegates later banned this practice. The article states as follows;

> "Critically, the ban was not limited to gifts that were provided with the expectation of a specific action in return. It was a blanket prohibition, for 'we expect that gifts lead to some warmth and generosity toward the giver' as Ms Teachout puts it, and these feelings could 'interfere with (the recipients) responsibility to put the country's interest first'. The framers,

> she writes, sought to move the United States away from the culture of gift-giving."[2]

In the Wall Street Journal in the June 7,8, 2014 weekend edition Barton Swain in reviewing Daniel Schulman's Book *Sons of Wichita* states as follows;

> "The well off have always drawn heavily on their bank accounts to move public policies and public opinion in a preferred direction; some buy newspapers (Robert McCormick, William Randolph Hearst); others get elected to office (the Kennedys, Michael Bloomberg), and a few just seem to enjoy the adventure of spending truckloads on elections they have little chance of winning (Linda McMahon, Ross Perot)."[3]

The potential severity of the problem is illustrated by the fact that "money" can also spill over to affect our judicial system. In the June 30, 2014 edition of Barrons, Skip Kaltenheuser in his article entitled "The Price of Justice" stated that a poll conducted by 20/20 Insight last year found that 9 of 10 American voters thought both direct contributions and independent spending affected courtroom decisions. This was as follows;

> "Earlier polls have consistently shown citizens losing confidence in the courts. Other polls show sizable cohorts of state judges and justices believing decisions are affected. It's not just past contributors calling the tunes. It's anticipation of getting contributions in the future, perhaps in a run for a higher court, as well as chilling fear of being attacked by well-financed opponents."[4]

Peter Schweizer in his 2013 book *Extortion (*Houghton Mifflin Harcourt) also notes that politicians also seek out money sources as they are aware of their power to get donations. The book summary as written on the inside cover states as follows;

> "Conventional wisdom holds that Washington is broken because outside special interests bribe politicians. The reverse is true: politicians have developed a new set of brass-knuckle legislative tactics designed to extort wealthy industries and

donors into forking over big donations—cash that lawmakers often funnel into the pockets of their friends and family. Ever wonder why Congress proposes boatloads of bills when so few ever become law? Answer; the real purpose of legislation is to strong-arm donations out of those with the most to lose from a bill's passage or defeat. And what about all those phone book-sized bills politicians propose, larded with indecipherable jargon? As it turns out, there is a new underground Washington industry made up of former lawmakers and staffers who reap millions from businesses needing help navigating the complex mess those politicians intentionally create. Until now, Washington's extortion racket has gone unreported. Yet thanks to an extraordinary effort by Peter Schweizer and the investigative research staff of the Government Accountability Institute, we now know the racketeering methods and the players who profit from them."[5]

Thus, it should not be surprising that our lawmakers are loaded; 35% are millionaires! In an October 27, 2014 Barron's article entitled "The Money Bags in Congress" Jim McTague stated this fact as follows;

"Almost There! The midterm elections are a little over a week away........... . Nevertheless, it's safe to say that regardless who wins, deep-pocketed Americans of all political persuasions will be amply represented in next year's Congress. Our lawmakers are loaded! There are 189 millionaires out of 538 members according to an analysis of financial data by Roll Call. That's 35%—an impressive concentration of wealth few country clubs can beat."[6]

If the problem wasn't confusing enough, the recent U.S. Supreme Court case of *Citizens United* has exacerbated the situation. A recent review of Ken Vogel's book *Big Money* by Bart Swaim as reported in the June 6th, 2014 edition of the Wall Street Journal stated as follows;

"Mr. Vogel's book suggests that these decisions—one by the Supreme Court in *Citizens United v. Federal Election Commission* and the other by a federal appeals court in *SpeechNow.org v. Federal Election Commission*—allow megadonors to dilute the power of both official campaigns and political parties in presidential elections. In short, these rulings held that organizations other than political campaigns have the First Amendment right to spend and say what they want in support of or in opposition to any political candidate they choose."[7]

Even President Obama in February 2012 at a fundraiser for his campaign in Medina, Washington remarked on the *Citizens United* decision as follows;

> "You now have the potential of 200 people deciding who ends up being elected president every single time. .... I may be the last presidential candidate who could win the way I won, which was coming out without a lot of special-interest support, without a handful of big corporate supporters, who was able to mobilize and had the time and the space to mobilize a grassroots effort, and then eventually got a lot of big donors, but started off small and was able to build. I think the capacity for somebody to do that is going to be much harder. In this election, I will be able to, hopefully, match whatever check the Koch brothers want to write. But I'm an incumbent president who already had this huge network of support all across the country and millions of donors. I'm not sure that the next candidate after me is going to be able to compete in that same way".[8]

Newt Gingerich in his book *To Save America* on page 115 and 116 explains why it is beneficial and practical for corporations to participate in the "quid pro quo game" in order to change the rules to their favor as follows;

> "Here is a more accurate narrative: big business knows the greatest threat to its survival is not governmental regulation, but competition from smaller, more innovative firms. So when the opportunity arises to cooperate with government in crafting new regulations to insulate themselves from competitive pressures or to secure economic benefits not provided competitors, big business lobbyists don't oppose the reforms; instead, they help write the laws to maximize their own advantage. It makes sense. Competition in the marketplace is hard. It's much easier to beat your competitors by using money and influence in Washington, D.C., to change the rules and regulations in your favor."[9]

The Wall Street Journal on August 1, and 2, 2015 reported that huge amounts of money are already starting to fund the 2016 Presidential campaign as follows;

> "Billionaires are bankrolling the early days of the 2016 presidential race to an unprecedented degree, with at least 40 of the wealthiest Americans plowing $60 million into super PACS aligned with the top tier of candidates"[10]

Ann Lee, a professor of finance at New York University wrote a book on how the U.S. can learn from China's recent success. In it she comments on how this money influence problem has turned off many American voters from voting because of their belief that they have no ability to change government. At page 59 she states as follows;

> "The view that the political system has become dysfunctional through the capture of special interests is well documented in books such as *Kabuki Democracy* by Eric Alterman. Professor Lawrence Lesig of Harvard University asserts that American politicians who get elected are really front men for large corporate or other special interests who funnel large amounts of money to their campaigns. Rather than represent the public interest, these politicians merely ensure that their patrons are satisfied with their voting records on particular issues."[11]

As noted earlier, I have taken measures to attack this problem in my political campaigns for the Presidency. Despite the recent Supreme Court rulings such as *Citizens United*, which could allow me to solicit large donations and to try to pose as front men for corporations, I have self-funded my campaign on a mere 5000 dollar budget!

Chapter 8

Reforming Our Government with the Independent Movement

The 3 preceding chapters discussed causes or reasons for the decline in America. As a result of these serious governmental problems, "we the people" of America have a very limited role or say in our futures. But we fortunately, as Americans are not forced to live with bad government. In fact, for years I believe us American voters have recognized the need to reform our current governmental system. Similarly, many experts or leading advocates have proposed needed changes in various forms. Indeed the Declaration of Independence states that the people have the absolute right to change our government, keep it limited and to protect our rights. It states as follows;

> "We hold these truths to be self-evident, that all men are created equal that they are endowed by their creator with certain unalienable rights, that among these are life, liberty and the pursuit of happiness. That to secure these rights, Governments are instituted among Men, deriving their just powers from the consent of the governed,--That whenever any Form of Government becomes destructive of these ends, it is the Right of the People to alter or to abolish it, and to institute new Government, laying its foundation on such

principles and organizing its powers in such form, as to them shall seem most likely to effect their Safety and Happiness."[1]

Therefore, as our 2015 system or form of government is ineffectively working or functioning in America, we the people have the right to, and must change it so once again as was the case with our founding fathers "the people control the government".

In Michael Reagan's book the *New Reagan Revolution,* (2011, St. Martins Griffin) he indicates his dad Ronald Reagan was fully aware of the need to build a coalition of a unified government. At page xiii of the forward of the book, it stated as follows;

"In all his major speeches, Ronald Reagan reached out not only to Republicans, but to Democrats and Independents. Being a 'recovering Democrat himself, President Reagan understood that he needed to build a transpartisan majority in order to govern America effectively. In the 1984 election, fully one-third of Ronald Reagan's support came from registered Democrats. Reagan reveals how his father attracted Democrats and built winning coalitions—and how we can do it again in the twenty-first century. When Ronald Reagan gave his show-stopping speech in 1976, he said, I believe the Republican Party has a platform that is a banner of bold, unmistakable colors, with no pastel shades'. He understood that the American people are tired of deciding between 'the lesser of two evils' every time they go to the polls. They want a true choice."[2]

Though Reagan's goals were admirable, and he had some success, nevertheless, he was still handcuffed by the two party system. The opposite party was for the most part forced to not go along with his agenda.

The 2009 Tea Party movement also shows an example of the need to reform our government and an effort to accomplish that, showing the American people's courage of rejecting the establishment and sticking up for freedom at the risk of fracturing the Republican party. Also, the Boston Tea Party of 1773 showed an act of defiance against the British authority whose judges, bureaucrats and politicians disrespected free Englishmen and their independence.

Jesse Ventura set forth this fact in his 2010 book *American Conspiracies, Lies, Lies and more Dirty Lies that the Government Tells Us* (Skyhorse Publishing, with Dick Russell).

At page 93, he set forth the need to separate from this 2 party addiction as follows;

> "In order to climb the ladder of the two political parties in our current system, you have to condone their corruption. I believe most people, when they initially start in politics, are good people. They come into the system wanting to do their job, to change things. But the longer you stay in the system, the more corrupt you become. The two parties to me are today no different than joining the Hell's Angels: Once an Angel, always an Angel.
> That's what holds true for Democrats or Republicans—unless you separate from them and join a third party movement, knowing that you've broken and beaten the addiction." [3].

Thomas Friedman, writing on the Opinion pages of the New York Times on October 2, 2010 wrote an article "There's a Third Party Rising" and concluded as follows;

> "We need a third party on the stage of the next presidential debate to look Americans in the eye and say 'These two parties are lying to you'. They can't tell you the truth because they are each trapped in decades of special interests. I am not going to tell you what you want to hear. I am going to tell you what you need to hear if we want to be the world's leaders, not the new Romans".[4]

Larry Diamond, who is a Stanford University political scientist discusses the inflexible, stagnant or rigid situation in our government today, which justifies government reform. He states that we have two bankrupt parties bankrupting the country as follows;

> "Indeed, our two-party system is ossified; it lacks integrity and creativity and any sense of courage or high-aspiration in confronting our problems. We simply will not be able to do the things we need to do as a country to move forward with all the vested interests that have accrued around these

two parties, added Diamond. They cannot think about the overall public good and the longer term anymore because both parties are trapped in short-term, zero-sum calculations, where each one's gains are seen as the others losses."[5]

THE INDEPENDENT SOLUTION

What I believe is the needed solution to America's decline and the best way to reform our dysfunctional government (as stated above) is for voters to vote as or declare themselves as "independents". This change can be stated in many different ways, such as "organize as independents, associate as independents, endorse or affiliate as independents, or join the independents movement". The common meaning to all of these terms is that you are simply abandoning the Republican and Democrats current 2 party system. As there are no rules for independents you now are not confined to supporting the party bosses commands, you pay no mandatory dues or make no expected contributions.

Wikipedia defines and discusses an independent politician as follows;

"An independent or nonpartisan politician is an individual *politician* not affiliated to any *political party*. There are numerous reasons why someone may stand for office as an independent. Independents may hold a *centrist* viewpoint between those of major political parties. Sometimes they hold a viewpoint more extreme than any major party, have an ideology comprising ideas from both sides of the political spectrum, or may have a viewpoint based on issues that they do not feel that any major party addresses.

Other independent politicians may be associated with a political party, be former members of it, or have views that align with it, but choose not to stand under its label. Others may belong to or support a political party but believe they should not formally represent it and thus be subject to its policies."[6]

A coalition, as used by Ronald Reagan is defined by dictionary.com as follows; "an alliance or union between groups, factions, or parties, especially for some temporary and specific reason"[7] Thus, I believe the coalition for independents should focus on the broad goal, purpose or reason to return the government back to the people, as designed by our founding fathers.

While this anti-major party movement is still in its infant stages and difficult to define with precision, I will set forth in the next 2 chapters more details on its nature. Chapter 9 will specify that despite much resistance from the major parties, the U.S. Supreme Court has on numerous occasions ruled that independents are legitimate. Chapter 10 will illustrate the growing movement of independents by showing that there now exists a national organization called independentvoters.org which has as its purpose to unite participants. This is especially helpful for those who wish to interact with other independents and desire their comaraderie or fellowship.

Chapter 9

The Independents Association

This Chapter will review what the United States Supreme Court has said about "independents" in the past 50 years. While it is a bit legalistic, this review is helpful as the Court elaborates on many themes in their decisions including;

1) The right to and the purposes of voters to go independent,
2) The many roles individuals can choose to play within such organizations, and
3) The continual attempts by the status quo or main parties to thwart these movements.

The U.S. Supreme Court nearly 50 years ago declared that candidates and voters have a choice as to whether they want to associate with any of the major political parties. In the case of *Storer v. Brown* 415 U.S. 724 (1974) our nation's highest Court set forth that in;

> "*Williams v. Rhodes*, 393 U.S. 23 (1968), the Court held that, although the citizens of a State are free to associate with one of the two major political parties, to participate in the nomination of their chosen party's candidates for public office and then to cast their ballots in the general election, the State must also provide feasible means for other political parties and other candidates to appear on the general election

> ballot. The Ohio law under examination in that case made no provision for independent candidates, and the requirements for any but the two major parties qualifying for the ballot were so burdensome that it was 'virtually impossible' for other parties, new or old, to achieve ballot position for their candidates. Page 415 U.S. 729."[1]

Decades later, the U.S. Supreme Court in the case of *Norman v. Reed* 502 U.S. 279 (1992) restated the right of like minded voters to gather for political reasons or ends at page 288 as follows;

> "For more than two decades, this Court has recognized the constitutional right of citizens to create and develop new political parties. The right derives from the First and Fourteenth Amendments and advances the constitutional interest of like-minded voters to gather in pursuit of common political ends, thus enlarging the opportunities of all voters to express their own political prferences. See *Anderson v. Celebreeze* 460 U.S. 780, 793-794 (1983);.....(citations omitted)."[2]

One reason for allowing new or independents to get ballot access is that the 2 major parties may not cover all the issues voters want to see on the ballot. The Fourth Circuit in the case of *Cromer v. The State of South Carolina,* 917 F 2d 819 (1990) at paragraph 18 stated the high value of having alternatives to the major parties as follows;

> "While one of the electoral interests which states may protect by reasonable regulation is that of the integrity of established and formally recognized major political parties, these may not extend to the effective exclusion of independent (and new party) candidacies, which serve important safety valve purposes not adequately served by major party candidacies alone, or by the availability of write-in candidacies"[3]

In the case of *Tashjian v. Republican Party of Connecticut* 479 U.S. 208 (1986) the Supreme Court elaborated on the nature of the right of the freedom to associate with any organization based on political beliefs as follows;

> "The nature of appellees' First Amendment interest is evident. It is beyond debate that freedom to engage in association for the advancement of beliefs and ideas is an inseparable aspect of the 'liberty' assured by the Due Process Clause of the Fourteenth Amendment, which embraces freedom of speech........ The freedom of association protected by the First and Fourteenth Amendments includes partisan political organization......... The right to associate with the political party of one's choice is an integral part of the basic constitutional freedom.....(citations omitted)"[4]

This *Tashjian* case further went on to state that within a major political party (this would also hold true for any political association) there are many various roles individuals could choose to play as follows;

> "A major state political party necessarily includes playing a broad spectrum of roles in the organization's activities. Some of the Party's members devote substantial portions of their lives to furthering its political and organizational goals, others provide substantial financial support, while still others limit their participation to casting their votes for some or all of the Party's candidates. Considered from the standpoint of the Party itself, the act of formal enrollment or public affiliation with the party is merely one element in the continuum of participation in Party affairs, and need not be in any sense the most important."[5]

In the U.S. Supreme Court case of *Eu v.S.F. County Democratic Central Committee* 489 U.S. 214 (1989) the Court stated in paragraph 15 that this freedom of association is broad, and includes choosing where you want to belong, and choosing its members and officers as follows;

> "Barring political parties from endorsing and opposing candidates not only burdens their freedom of speech but also infringes upon their freedom of association. It is well settled that partisan political organizations enjoy freedom of association protected by the First and Fourteenth Amendments. Association means not only that an individual voter has the right to associate with the political party of her choice... but also that a political party has a right to 'identify

> the people who constitute the association' and to select a 'standard bearer who best represents the parties ideologies and preferences' (citations omitted)."[6]

Despite that the Supreme Court clearly ruled that new parties or independents have a right to organize, this same Court has repeatedly dealt with legislatures (especially in Ohio) attempting to abolish their rights, or to continue the monopoly of the major parties. This discriminatory practice of Ohio politics and the nature of this subject was set forth in the case of *Williams v. Rhodes* 393 U.S. 23 in Section III as follows;

> "No extended discussion is required to establish that the Ohio laws before us give the two old, established parties a decided advantage over any new parties struggling for existence thus place substantially unequal burdens on both the right to vote and the right to associate. The right to form a party for the advancement of political goals means little if a party can be kept off the election ballot and thus denied an equal opportunity to win votes. So also, the right to vote is heavily burdened if that vote may be cast only for one of two parties at a time when other parties are clamoring for a place on the ballot. In determining whether the State has power to place such unequal burdens on minority groups where rights of this kind are at stake, the decisions of this Court have consistently held that only a compelling state interest in the regulation of a subject within the State's constitutional power to regulate can justify limiting First Amendment freedoms'".[7]

In this landmark case of *Williams v. Rhodes* 393 U.S. 23 the Supreme Court scolded the State of Ohio further for this monopolistic practice at Section III as follows;

> "The fact is, however, that the Ohio system does not merely favor a two party system, it favors two particular parties, the Republicans and the Democrats—and, in effect, tends to give them a complete monopoly. There is, of course, no reason why two parties should retain a permanent monopoly on the right to have people vote for or against them. Competition in ideas and governmental policies is at the core of our electoral process and of the First Amendment freedoms. New parties

> struggling for their place must have the time and opportunity to organize in order to meet reasonable requirements for ballot position, just as the old parties had in the past."[8]

In summation, it is clear that the U.S. Supreme Court has ruled that anyone has the right to not belong to the major Republican and Democratic parties and that they can associate or organize their political beliefs in a manner to their liking and they can partake in roles in support therein to their own choosing.

The Court has continually scolded states, especially Ohio for their past efforts to force voters to vote for or against only Republicans or Democrats. As was stated in the case of *Anderson v. Celebreeze* 460 U.S. 780 at page 794 is as follows;

> "It discriminates against those candidates and—of particular importance—against those voters whose political preferences lie outside the existing political parties. By limiting the opportunities of independent-minded voters to associate in the electoral arena to enhance their political effectiveness as a group, such restrictions threaten to reduce diversity and competition in the marketplace of ideas. Historically, political figures outside the two major parties have been fertile sources of new ideas and new programs; many of their challenges to the *status quo* have, in time, made their way into the political mainstream. .... In short, the primary values protected by the First Amendment--'a profound national commitment to the principle that on public issues should be uninhibited, robust, and wide-open' are served when election campaigns are not monopolized by the existing political parties". (citations omitted).[9]

Chapter 10

Independentvoters.org

As was noted in the prior Chapter we all have the legal right to associate freely in regards to our political beliefs and ideas. And as was noted in Chapter 3, I did just that by running for President as an independent in 2008, and 2012. Although at that time I wasn't aware of the political theory of such, I merely followed the rules as told to me by the Secretary of State of Ohio. I was aware, however, that I did not agree with the major parties' beliefs so I ran alone as a "non party candidate".

In the late months of 2014 I happened to "google independents" and came across a website entitled independentvoters.org. I was amazed to find out that there was something out there in regards to voters who did not want to align with the 2 party system. The possibility of having a support group peaked my interest, so I started to inquire into this group. I looked up the definition of association and it stated "an organized body of people who have an interest, activity or purpose in common"(American Heritage Dictionary).[1] I will devote this chapter to this association which has its purpose of abandoning the 2 major parties. From this discussion, the reader will become informed as to its nature.

I called the New York City phone number and they referred me to the Ohio President Cynthia Carpathios. She welcomed me and referred me to their website which contained an Ohio organizational statement. She also referred me to the national website which set forth a multiple page discussion on their history and mission. The nature of these organizations will be set forth below.

In *Ohio*, this organization is affiliated with IndependentVoting.org., a national strategy and organizing center for the Independent movement. Independent Ohio is grassroots and is building a movement and supporting structural political reforms that allows the political process to open up to independents and to try to reduce partisanship in government. Independent Ohio focuses on empowering voters by building a collective voice and hoping to reform Ohio's politically process by giving them a stronger voice. The organization reaches out to other states in the midwest and has them participate on their conference calls. The website of Independent Ohio states as follows;

> "Our nation is self-governing; this means that elected officials and civil servants work for the American people through their oath of office to the Constitution. All decisions of our government at every level should reflect loyalty to our nation and to the American People—not to political parties, party bosses, campaign contributors or other special interests The American People ("we the people") should be the owners of America's electoral process.
>
> Ideas should be judged based on the reason and evidence that support them, not on the party or politician who proposes them. Independents are united on these core values and support one another in advancing them through structural political reform, even though they may respectfully disagree on substantive policies."[2]

The *National* organization was formerly part of the CUIP. It has as its mission to be a national communications and organizing center for the greater than 40% of Americans who identify themselves as independents. It seeks to be a movement to reform partisanship politics in America. They do not seek to be another special interest but hope to turn around the regressive influence of partisan politics. They claim to have played a big part in the election of President Obama. Independent Voting.org hopes to end closed primaries which they claim excludes unfairly independent voters from primaries. They also seek to end the partisan control of redistricting and the exclusion of independents from the televised presidential debates. They argue that independents need a voice because the Constitution never made mention of parties and that George Washington even warned us that these factions could become destructive in nature. They also argue the parties operate in a closed system where they make all the rules and virtually make up all the representatives in our government agencies. Therefore, they can keep out competition and to sustain their own power or monopoly.

The Committee for a Unified Party(CUIP) was founded in 1994 by veteran community organizers and third-party activists. They founded the Reform Party which was short-term lived. CUIP like IndependentVoting. org. work to bring about structural reforms which allow the American people to participate more directly in the political and policymaking process. They both have an online presence and focus on grassroots organizing of unorganized and unaffiliated independent voters.

The CUIP gets its funding from thousands of individual donors in all 50 states. They do not endorse or campaign for candidates. However, they give tactical support, for example in the 2004 election cycle, they initiated Choosing an Independent Presidential (ChIP), a project in which voter groups within the national network screened specially presidential candidates. In 2008, they repeated the process and many activist groups joined in with the Obama campaign.

The network of independent voters extends to about 40 states and some of the activities on a grassroots level include local discussion groups and statewide conference calls. The website states as some of their activities as follows;

> "Developing reform legislation and meeting with and lobbying state legislators, testifying at legislative hearings, public education through writing letters to the editor and op-ed pieces in local newspapers and working on a range of local political reform efforts. Every six weeks CUIP's president, Jackie Salit, hosts a national conference call for new and veteran political activists. One hundred and fifty leaders from as many as 40 states participate in each of these conference calls, making them the largest regular gathering of independent voters in the country."[3]

I read over these materials and started to listen in on the conference calls. The organization heavily promoted the national bi-yearly convention in New York City on March 14th, 2015 at New York University. I thought going to this would be very helpful to get a feel for the movement. At first, I booked a pricy hotel for 3 nights, but I later decided to go on a budget trip as I was uncertain as to the value of this event. I ended up staying at the Hotel Carter near 42nd Street and Broadway which had direct access to a strip club. Oh well, after all this was the "Big Apple"! I spent the night before and after the convention on a Cleveland to New York City greyhound express bus.

I arrived at the reception the night before and found a hundred plus people jammed into a small office space occupied by the Open Primaries organization. I quickly tried to meet as many people as possible and I jotted down their names and where they were from and anything interesting that they told me. At the Saturday convention, I arrived early to try to meet more attendees. I found out that the guests were from many states, especially California, Arizona, Florida and New York. I received a program in which Jackie Salit set forth a message. The brochure stated as follows;

> "Thus, the new dawn of a new century ushered in an explosive new 'fact on the ground'-namely that more and more Americans from all walks of life were becoming independents. We faced this new reality with gusto, ... our emphasis became organizing independent voters without a party, and the project known as IndependentVoting.Org was born. The demand for strategies and grassroots efforts that turned away from the parties, including minor parties, and towards systematic reform that empowered independent voters-42% of the country was growing."[4]

Panelists were on stage and they discussed various questions as raised by President Salit. Video clips illustrated a few candidates who won their political offices running as an independent, such as Angus King, a previous governor of the State of Maine.

Of particular interest to me was the question and answer period where attendees posed questions to the panel. A variety of attendees asked questions including a homeless person, lawyers, Richard Winger, a ballot access expert, a lady with a development disability, a lady from the tea party, a Plaintiff in a case involving independent voters issues and local politicians.

Likewise, the issues raised were varied from income inequality, to whether the organization should run candidates?, to what can independents do to help out the cause? A common theme to every point was that the existing 2 party system was doing little or nothing to help them out.

So overall, I thought the convention was a worthwhile experience and quite fascinating. I was now convinced that I had companions to travel with if I wanted. I was also convinced once again that America needed to reform its political system. Harry Kresky is the attorney for independentvoters. org.. He made a terse statement which I found amusing at the convention, "anything that takes flesh off the republicans or democrats is a good thing". President Jackie Salit made a comment about kicking them in the teeth.

However, after the convention some concerns or questions remained. The first is whether independentvoters.org. do or should endorse, or sponsor candidates? As was stated on their website the answer was no. Also, President Salit stated no at the convention due to past problems that they encountered.. However, many attendees wanted them to do so and were disappointed with Salit's answer. Peter White, from New Hampshire, at the convention was conducting an informal survey as to who the people wanted to run for President in 2016 as an Independent. So, therefore, from a practical standpoint, does this organization lose a lot of its effectiveness from not endorsing candidates? As was noted in Chapter 10, "the right to form a party for the advancement of political goals means little if a party can be kept off the election ballot".

A second question or concern I have is in regards to the "top 2 issue" or similarly called the "open primary issue". I noticed at the convention that this seemed to be the major theme or item on their agenda. California and Washington have voted this in and a few states are trying to get it in. Prior to me going to the convention, Richard Winger, the ballot access expert from San Francisco sent me an email which alerted me to his belief that the top 2 system ruins independent candidates!5

With the top 2 system as I understand it, only 2 candidates ever go to the ballot in the general election. Everyone faces off in the primary election, and the top two vote receivers move on. Thus, if you run as an independent you can no longer run in the general election unless you run in the primary and get the most votes or second place. Winger's email set forth many examples as to how the top two ruins independents. He states that it almost always has the effect of producing general elections with only Democrats and Republicans on the ballot. For example, he cites that 116 minor party candidates ran for office in top 2 primaries and in each one did not win enough votes to advance to the general election. His email also stated that;

> "If the U.S. had a top-two system for president in 2008, Hillary Clinton and Barack Obama would have been the only candidates allowed to run for president in November. They each got over 17,500,000 presidential primary votes. But no Republican polled as much as 10,000,000 votes, because

> the Republican field was split up among McCain, Ron Paul, Huckabee, Romney and Giuliani".[5]

Thus, at this point I agree with Richard Winger. In the present system it is still possible for independents to get in the general election if they meet the state's requirements. I did in 2008 and again in 2012. If top 2 existed in Ohio it would have been virtually impossible for me to do so because I am a newcomer with a growing support base. The Republicans and Democrats have been around for a hundred years with millions of party members! Furthermore, the general election is the main event for voting. I believe the primaries were only designed to winnow down candidates within their respective parties, prior to the main event. Furthermore, it doesn't seem fair for non-party members to be voting for or against candidates in a party they have no real interest in. Thus, I cannot see the point in moving up election day six months earlier.

When I was at the convention, I began to question the top 2 system and a staff official from open primaries told me Richard Winger was "a pain in the ass". I asked an official from Arizona, where the top 2 system is being proposed soon to the voters, about its benefits. He could not give me a reasonable explanation. A thought popped into my mind. Are the major parties behind this somehow in an attempt to sabotage independents or minor parties? After all, this is politics and it can get dirty!

In conclusion, my affiliation with independentvoters.org thus far has been beneficial and has broadened my knowledge on the movement to abandon the 2 party system.

Chapter 11

Independents and the Coalition for Independent Voters (C F I V) Will Save America and Reform Our Government

This book has shown that while America has for centuries been the greatest country in the world, there are credible signs of its decline. As I showed in Chapters 5 through 7, I believe these problems are government related and that they involve a massively overblown bureaucratic system based on socialistic principles which are a far cry from the limited government established by our founding fathers. Furthermore, the legislatures and other government members now often place their parties desire to win and outside money influences above their obligation to benefit the public's interest. I looked up the definition of "morass" and I believe it accurately describes the nature of our government today;

- complicated or confused situation;
- disordered or muddled situation or circumstance;
- one that impedes progress;
- overwhelms; (Merriman Webster and Free Dictionary).[1]

Therefore, the continuation of this present system is almost certain to result in regression or collapse.

Thus, as I have stated throughout this book, is the point that we must go back to "free people controlling the limited government"; a needed government reform. In the last 3 chapters of this book I proposed that the independent voter's movement or association may be our only hope toward accomplishing this goal. Even if it takes years and if it takes a piece by piece dismantling of the existing morass, it is more likely to result in more benefits than to allow the status quo to remain unchallenged. I believe benefits will start showing up shortly once the major parties realize we are serious. We must simply abandon the 2 party system which does not benefit us.

It has been many years since I heard my father's preachings, my 31 point game for the Cardinal Huskies, becoming Mount Union College's freshmen vice president and now a few years since getting 12,557 Presidential votes. But today I believe the time is ripe for all Americans to unite, stand up tall and not be silenced and claim "we are too big to fail!" We must shout out to the Republicans and Democrats and to all the government bureaucrats, under the independent banner of our forefathers, in the famous words of my father "WE'RE NOT GONNA TAKE IT!"

While I fully support every independent and the independentvoters.org movement which I discussed in Chapter 10, I noted that there are some differences that I can not fully endorse.

Therefore, I have initiated an association or organization called the Coalition For Independent Voters (C.F.I.V.) to which I have appointed myself founder and President for the time being. Any personal donations can be mailed to Richard Duncan at 1100 East Blvd, Aurora, Ohio 44202 to help with administrative costs. Any correspondences can be emailed to *duncanforpresident@hotmail.com*.

Any help would be greatly appreciated.

GOOD LUCK AMERICA! GOD BLESS!
RICHARD A. DUNCAN

NOTES

PROLOGUE

1. Michael Reagan, *New Reagan Revolution,* (St. Martins Griffin, 2011).
2. Bill Clinton, *Back To Work In The Future Business,* (Knopf Publishing, 2011).
3. David M. Walker, *Comeback America: Turning The Country Around And Restoring Fiscal Responsibility*, (New York: Random House, 2009) p. 36-37.
4. Michael Reagan, op. Cit.
5. Chris Mathews, *Jack Kennedy Elusive Hero,* (Simon and Schuster, 2012).
6. Ronald Reagan, *Acceptance Speech at the 1980 Republican Convention, July 17, 1980*
7. Newt Gingerich, *To Save America*, (Regnery Publishing, 2010).

CHAPTER 1

DREAMS OF MY FATHER AND MY TEEN AND COLLEGE YEARS

1. Irvin Weaver, 1971 poem written at Cardinal High School.
2. *Dyanamo,* Mount Union College weekly newspaper.

CHAPTER 2

THE REAGAN 1980'S AND MY LEGAL EDUCATION

1. *Duncan v. Middlefield* 23 O.S. 3d 83

CHAPTER 3

MY RUN FOR THE WHITE HOUSE

1. John Horton, "Duncan for President? Aurora man in the race", *Plain Dealer*
2. Bobby Cubertson letter to the Ohio Secretary of State, filed August 18, 2008.
3. Jeff Russ, *Daily Kent Stater,* November 4th, 2008.
4. http://www.Plunderbund.com., "Follow Up On Richard Duncan's Presidential Campaign," posted November 16, 2008.

CHAPTER 4

THE GOOD OLE U.S.A.

1. Michael Wines, "China Appears to be Moving to Halt Grass-Roots Candidates", *New York Times,* June 9, 2011.
2. Dinesh D'Souza, *America, Imagine A World Without Her,* (Regnery Publishing, 2014)
3. Daniel Walker Howe, *What Hath God Wrought* (New York:Oxford University Press, 2009) Angus Maddison, *The World Economy: Historical Statistics* (Paris OECD Press, 2003).
4. Bill Clinton, *Back To Work In The Future Business,* (Knopf Publishing, 2011).
5. Newt Gingerich, *To Save America,* (Regnery Publishing, 2010).
6. Gene Epstein, "Works for Squares", *Barrons,* September 1, 2014.
7. Janet Yellen, *Wall Street Journal,* October 18,19, 2014.
8. Chris Mathews, *Elusive Hero,* (Simon and Schuster, 2011).
9. Dinesh D'Souza, *Imagine A World Without Her,* (Regnery Publishing, 2014).
10. Fawaz Gerez, *Obama and the Middle East,*(London:Palgrave MacMillan, 2012) pp. 13, 152.

CHAPTER 5

TOO BIG OF GOVERNMENT AND SOCIALISM

1. Richard Epstein, *The Classical Liberal Constitution,* (Harvard University Press, 2014), as reviewed by Andrew Napolitano in *Barrons*, on August 2, 2014.

2. Heather Cox Richardson, *To Make Men Free,* (Basic Books, 2014), as reviewed by Lee Edwards in the *Wall Street Journal* September 20, 21, 2014.
3. Ann Coulter, *Demonic,* (Crown Forum, 2012).
4. George W. Bush, *Decision Points*, (Broadway Books, 2011).
5. The *Federalist,* No 84, May 28, 1788.
6. Martin Conrad, *Barrons,* March 23, 2015.
7. John Locke, excerpts from *Two Treatises of Government,* 1690, "John Locke's Theories Put into Practice," http://history.wisc.edu/sommerville/367/locke%20decindep.htm.
8. Rowan Scarborough, "George Soros' Liberal Agenda Will Carry Weight in Obama Presidency" *Human Events*, November 5, 2008, http://www.humanevents.com/article.php?id=29359.
9. Dinesh D'Souza, *America, Imagine A World Without Her,* (Regnery Publishing, 2014).
10. Ibid
11. Dinesh D'Souza, *OBama's America,* (Washington D.C. Regnery, 2012) pg. 67-90.
12. Benjamin Powell, *Out of Poverty, Sweatshops In The Global Economy,* (Cambridge University Press, 2015), as reviewed by Gene Epstein in *Barrons* March 2, 2015.
13. "A Blighted Decade", by Scott Bullock and Nick Sibilla, in *Barron's,* July 6, 2015.

CHAPTER 6

THE REPUBLICAN/DEMOCRAT 2 PARTY SYSTEM PROBLEM

1. Bill Clinton, *Back To Work In The Future Business,* (Knopf Publishing, 2011).
2. Joe Lieberman, "Can We Stop the Partisan Polarization That Is Crippling Our Government?" speech given November 20th, 2013 at Roanoke College as reported by Tiffany Holland.
3. Steve LaTourette, as reported by Record Publishing on March 6, 2013 by Conner Howard.
4. James McCarty, *Cleveland Plain Dealer,* September 23, 2011.
5. Chris Mathews, *Jack Kennedy, Elusive Hero*, (Simon and Shuster, 2012).

CHAPTER 7

MONEY INFLUENCE

1. Wikepedia
2. Zephyr Teachout, *Corruption In America,* (Harvard Publishing, 2014), as reviewed by Sarah Chayes, Wall Street Journal, September 27,28, 2014 weekend edition.
3. Daniel Schulman, *Sons of Wichita,* (Grand Central Publishing, 2015), as reviewed by Barton Swain, Wall Street Journal, June 7,8, 2014 weekend edition.
4. Skip Kaltenheuser, *Barrons,* June 30, 2014 in his article "The Price of Justice".
5. Peter Schweizer, *Extortion,* (Houghton Mifflin Harcourt, 2013).
6. Jim McTaque, *Barrons*, October 27, 2014, "The Money Bags in Congress".
7. Ken Vogel, *Big Money*, as reviewed by Bart Swaim, Wall Street Journal, June 6th, 2014 edition.
8. Barack Obama, speech at a fundraiser in February 2012 in Medina Washington.
9. Newt Gingerich, *To Save America,* (Regnery Publishing, 2010).
10. *The Wall Street Journal*, Saturday/Sunday, August 1-2, 2015, page A4.
11. *What The U.S. Can Learn From China*, Ann Lee,(Brett-Koehler Publishing, 2012).

CHAPTER 8

REFORMING OUR GOVERNMENT WITH THE INDEPENDENT MOVEMENT

1. Declaration of Independence
2. Michael Reagan, *The New Reagan Revolution,* (St. Martins Griffin, 2011).
3. Jesse Ventura, *American Conspiracies, Lies, Lies and More Dirty Lies, That The Government Tells Us,* with Dick Russell, (Skyhorse Publishing, 2010).
4. Thomas Friedman, "There's a Third Party Rising" New York Times Opinion Page October 2, 2010.
5. Larry Diamond, Stanford University Political Scientist, quote is from an interview by Thomas Friedman, Ibid.
6. Wikepedia

7. Dictionary.com

CHAPTER 9

THE INDEPENDENTS ASSOCIATION

1. *Storer v. Brown* 415 U.S. 724 (1974)
2. *Norman v. Reed* 502 U.S. 279 (1992)
3. *Cromer v. The State of South Carolina* 917 F. 2d 819 (1990)
4. *Tashjian v. Republican Party of Connecticut*, 479 U.S. 208 (1986)
5. Ibid
6. *Eu vs. S.F. County Democratic Central Committee*, 489 U.S. 214 (1989)
7. *Williams v. Rhodes* 393 U.S. 23 (1968)
8. Ibid.
9. *Andersen v. Celebreeze* 460 U.S. 780 (1983)

CHAPTER 10

INDEPENDENTVOTERS.ORG

1. *American Heritage Dictionary of the English Language* 5th Ed. 2011 Houghton Mifflin Publishing Corp.
2. www.independentohio.org
3. *independentVoting.org*
4. *Partnerships For Independent Power*, Jacqueline Salit, Program at the 2015 Convention of Independent Voters. New York University.
5. Richard Winger, Editor of Ballot Access News, personal email 6/1/15.

CHAPTER 11

HOW THE COALITION FOR INDEPENDENT VOTERS WILL SAVE AMERICA AND REFORM OUR GOVERNMENT

1. Merriman Webster and Free Dictionary

www.ingramcontent.com/pod-product-compliance
Lightning Source LLC
Chambersburg PA
CBHW030914180526
45163CB00004B/1834

* 9 7 8 1 5 0 3 5 8 8 1 9 6 *